# Journeys with God

## Guidance and Directions from Him

Carolyn J. Walton

WestBow Press books may be ordered through booksellers or by contacting:

WestBow Press
A Division of Thomas Nelson & Zondervan
1663 Liberty Drive
Bloomington, IN 47403
www.westbowpress.com
1 (866) 928-1240



ISBN: 978-1-5127-7067-4 (sc)
ISBN: 978-1-5127-7068-1 (hc)
ISBN: 978-1-5127-7066-7 (e)

Library of Congress Control Number: 2016921632

Print information available on the last page.

WestBow Press rev. date: 03/27/2017

# Contents

# DEDICATION

I dedicate this book to the young girls who have not seen or heard God's purpose in their lives. I pray you will humble yourself and let Him lead you to your purpose and keep you as you travel to obtain it. Remember, He never said it would be easy but He did say, "I will never leave nor forsake you".

I also dedicate this book to the chosen people. God chose you for His purpose. Seek God as you read these pages. I have poured out my fears, doubts, victories and defeats for you. I was led by the Holy Spirit to write this book and I believe it will be a blessing to you. Step out on faith even when it seems a little weird or crazy to you.

To my grandson, Makari, follow your dreams and pray to God for help with all your decisions. To my son, Carnell, live life to the fullest means to take advantage of the opportunities God gives you while you are young I love you. To my youngest grandson, Christion, I pray you are healthy, loving, anointed and full of love. To my daughter-in-law, make God your primary focus and watch Him do everything He promised to you.

To my Pastor and Co-Pastor, thanks for the encouragement and confirmations you gave me throughout my valleys, mountains, and wilderness. I pray that God continues to bless you at the training site. I know now that I am an ambassador of Jesus Christ. I represent the Body of Christ, the local church I attend and my biological family. I pray, I will represent them well and godly.

To Angela Walton, thanks for the unconditional support you always offer. You are a great woman of God. Listen and do what He commands of you.

To the ones who sowed seeds for the book, thank you and may God bless you hundred-fold in health and substances. May God bless you and the works of your hands. I thank Minister Victoria for helping me through this faith journey.

Special thanks to my siblings who supported me on this journey. You are the tops! I thank Patricia for your help.

Last but not least, thanks Eric for all your support in the ministry.

# Journey to This Place

A journey with many lessons and mistakes
Mistakes which gave more strength and knowledge
More wisdom and understanding
More love and patience
A journey which revealed a purpose
A purpose for such a time as this
A purpose more powerful than one could think of
A journey only God could direct and ordain
A journey only God could sustain
A journey to His holy place

# History

I was reared in a small city. It was six children in the household and two adults. I was treated well as a child. I knew I was loved and taken care of. My life consisted of church, school, and family outings. I had only one sister in the home with me. Later I found out that I had more sisters from the absent parent. Growing up in the 60's and 70's, I had an average childhood. I spent most of my time alone as much as I could with six siblings. I had only one close friend in school and a few associates.

I got picked on many times. They called me black and ugly. I heard it so much that I believed it. I could not maintain a healthy relationship because of my low self-esteem. I got good grades and was in the upper level classes in school but my self-esteem was very low. I know children call each other out their names but those names really stuck with me. At school, I felt the same way. I was not in the popular group. The other students talked with me when it was convenient for them but I was not a part of the group.

We have to understand that if a person is mean, it can come from their past. We are sometimes the product of our environment. The verbal abuse and curses can be passed down from parents. As I think about it today, I will say it could have been a lot worse.

I wanted to know more about my biological father. I remembered him coming to visit and giving my mom money for his children. My step dad did not want him to come to his house anymore so we did not see him again. I was upset about that because he gave up too easily and did not try to contact us. I believe he should have called and demanded his children meet over to his mother or sister's houses for a visit, he never did it. I had to forgive him and realized he did the best he could with his state of mind.

I felt my parents were strict on us. We could not go out to parties until we turned sixteen years old. We had to be in at 11 pm when we started dating. Most of the time, I felt alone and lonely. I always felt out of place, as if I did not belong there. My siblings reminded me that I was different from the others. They continued telling me that I was ugly and black. I knew I did not fit in with the rest. I look back now and see why I felt out of place. No matter where I went, I felt I did not belong there. I had a void inside of me that would not go away.

I loved to see my mother at home when I got out of school. I really adore my mother. With my personality, I had a problem with how she handled things. She was calm unless someone messed with her children. I felt she should have stood up more for herself. But now I see she took care of business the best way. She did not have to be loud or respond to others. She let things roll off her back and prayed about it.

I now have her strategy for handling issues. I just let it roll off most of the time. I pray and ask for directions from God. The answer to most situations is to show love and watch God work it out for me. I had to use spiritual weapons to fight the enemy. My weapons are prayer, praise, scriptures, confessions, and worship.

Back to my childhood and how I felt inside while I was growing up, I felt lonely and out of place. I remember an elder cousin died. I used to walk around alone and cry about her death. I knew her but I just held on to that sorrowful time to give me a reason to feel sad. It did not make sense to cry if nothing is wrong and most of the times I wanted to cry because I felt empty inside. I felt an emptiness that was hard to explain and I was not going to try to explain it to them. They probably would have thought I was losing my mind. I was already seeing things before it happened. I shared some of those visions with my siblings but they began to look at me strange. I stopped sharing those visions. I believed I was weird and did not belong with the family so why should I make them think I was crazy too? I kept secrets for example: I liked Bible study and going to church most of the time. Church was a test sometimes because I knew the behavior of the saints was not of God. I felt that the things the adults were doing was not pleasing to God. As a young adult, I did some of the same things I saw them do. I decided to just attend church and not work in the church if I was going to do the things that are not right.

One area in my life I was trained by my environment was the way I looked at men. I always saw husbands and boyfriends cheat on their wives and girlfriends and so I concluded that all men are not good. I decided to treat them bad before they treated me that way. I will admit that there were a couple of times I felt more than I wanted to feel for them. So unknowingly, I would destroy the relationship before they could hurt me. Later, when I wanted to try to stay in a relationship, I still felt unfulfilled. I would date more than one guy at a time so my whole "being" would be complete. For example, Jim was good as a provider, Jack was good for his humor, Jerry was good spiritually, and Jeff was good in bed. I made a whole man out of two or three guys. You get the picture. I was not sleeping with them all but I pulled from each person what I needed from them. I let them know that I was not serious and did not want to be committed. That did not go well with them or me. The void was still there!

When I was in the military, I thought about suicide often. I wanted to just forget about being in this world because I did not belong no matter where I lived. When I was young, I felt I did not belong with my family. I always felt differently. People were decent to me but I never connected with too many people. I always had only one close friend. People found it hard to believe that I had low self-esteem. I always acted as if I had it together but I did not have it half together. I learned that people with low self-esteem sometimes act aggressively to hide their true feelings.

Suddenly, I noticed that as I got older that I was still not satisfied within myself. I was still depressed and empty. I decided not to date and see if I would feel better. I got tired of the small relationships. I was still depressed and empty. Don't get me wrong, I had some great guys who treated me like a queen, but I was still feeling empty and out of place. After all these years, I blame it on my siblings. And then it happens! I had one relationship too many. He was a Bible carrying brother. He was cunning. After the last straw in that relationship, I found myself crying to God and asking Him what I should do about myself. I was tired of those relationships and wanted to be free. I still did not get it. It was not the relationships with men but the relationship with God.

God spoke to me so clear, I thought I could see Him in the house. The Spirit of God said that God called me to do His will. I found out that man cannot fill that empty space in me. God said that He made that space for Himself and not for man. A large space was within me and I could not do anything to fill that void. It was for God only. I was trying to put people, jobs, places, and much more in God's space. When I got up from that prayer, I was made whole that day. I felt complete inside. The space was filled with His Spirit. I had to surrender to Him. I remember the room became bright. I knew the presence of the Lord was there. I have never experienced His Spirit like that before that day. God touched me and filled me with His Power. I was never lonely again. I was never searching for something or someone to fill a void. I did not have a void anymore to fill. Men were going to fail me no matter what they did because I wanted them to take a place in me that God created for Him. God called that the "chosen" space. I am chosen and I had a void to be filled by Him.

Now the journey begins. Things do not just happen in our lives. God has put our directions in order. We have to let Him guide us. Even when we do not let Him guide us, He has a way to make it work out for our good if we love Him and are called for a purpose. Look at Roman 8:28 and get that Word. In other words, He can still get the glory. When you are chosen, God is continually calling you. He created you in a way that you cannot live a peaceful life without Him as the center of it.

# JOURNEY HOME FROM WORK

**May 3, 2010**

Rain, rain, rain.

There were warnings of tornadoes in the area. The ride home was long and rainy. As I thought about the trip I began to become weary. God started me looking at my journey with Him by using the situation I was in at the time.

I was in a storm at the time but I knew He was still there. The storm seems long and weary, like the ride home. But God let me see that, under each bridge, there was relief for a moment. Then back into the rain. I understood the spiritual aspect of this journey. I had to stay in the storm but I know that within it, some relief will come. I began to praise God. Then I began to ride the storm in a numb state. I had to keep pushing until I got home or until the storm passed. The storm began to be lighter and I made it home safe. I made sure I thanked God for His protection, guidance and safe travel from the water puddles and the fast trucks. I saw, or should I say, I noticed for a long time that I was on this side of the road alone. Many cars were on the other side. Now and then a car would come on my side of the road and then I am alone again. On this journey, I will see myself alone doing God's will but I had to keep going. Later, I noticed a car with it flashers on. He was being cautious all the way up the interstate. Some of us barely move because we are too cautious to make a move. I kept a safe speed. Some passed me and I even passed a couple of them. I stayed steady and firm in my speed. I did not stop until I reached my destination.

I had to encourage myself all the way home. I know I have to encourage myself on this journey also. I was physically tired when I got home. We will get tired and weary on this journey but we have to keep moving. Narrow is the road we travel on this journey.

**SCRIPTURES:**

Have I not commanded you? Be strong and courageous; do not be afraid, nor be dismayed, for the Lord your God is with you wherever you go. Joshua 1:9 (NKJV)

The eternal God is your refuge and underneath are the everlasting arms. Deuteronomy 33:27 (NKJV)

Thank you, God, for my journey today.

# A Day's Journey

## May 8, 2010

I am practicing for a praise service today.

I started thinking about a family trip. I am torn inside as to which way to go. Should I stay for rehearsal or should I go on the family trip? I used not having money as an excuse not to go but deep inside I know I had a struggle with going. What is the deal, I wonder? After offers were made to give me money, I rejected them. I decided to see if God would release the funds in a miraculous way so that I would know which way to go. I packed my bags just in case. After praying to God and asking for direction, I remembered the scripture about forsaking your mother and father to follow Jesus. Then a revelation came to me that I will be gone many times in the future and will not be able to attend family functions. I then surrendered to God. Lord, it is alright. I thought about the false hope and the lonely feeling and the disappointment. Now I see it spiritually; the journey with God is sometimes "Alone".

Just be still until He reveals. I started going and taking care of the ministry business. I had prices to check on and items to purchase for the ministry. Too much time has been used up already. The scriptures below reveal the message that God's way is perfect. Whichever way He sends me. I have to obey and praise Him for using me.

### Scripture:

As for God, His way is perfect; the word of the Lord is proven; He is a shield for all who trust in Him. II Samuel 22:31 (NKJV)

Thank You, God, for letting me know that a shift is going in my life which will be only for You. I need to ensure I do God's will rejoicing.

# Journey in My Mind

**May 21, 2010**

I keep thinking about the service and what has been taking place with the ministry. I am sure of some of the aspects of my life but everything is not clear to me yet. I see and do not understand. And what I understand, I hide in my heart. I need wisdom, direction, and spiritual insight that comes only from God.

Why, why do I feel like a hidden agenda is taking place? I feel disconnected from this place and not connected to the people. Each day starts with giving God praise and prayers for His mercy and grace. I drag myself out of bed but I had to drag my mind out first. Then I travel 42 miles to work. I am traveling each day and every moment without knowing who or what will be the direction for me that day. I just have to trust God and praise Him for protection and using me for His kingdom.

The evidence is there that God is still in charge. I see joy, hope, and faith restored. I hear laughter where there was no laughter. I feel peace within ones who had no peace. My mind goes on a journey each day but my spirit stays with You, Lord. I shall not be moved even when I do not understand. Correct what is wrong, Lord. Move anything that tries to destroy, delay or misdirect what You have for me. Let the rain and the sunshine in my daily life reflect Your goodness and Your blessings.

### Scriptures:

Give to the Lord the glory due His Name; bring an offering and come before Him. Oh, worship the Lord in the beauty of holiness! I Chronicles 16:29 (NKJV)

You therefore must endure hardship as a good soldier of Jesus Christ. No one engaged in warfare entangles himself with the affairs of this life, that he may please him who enlisted him as a soldier. II Timothy 2:3-4 (NKJV)

Thank You, Lord, for knowing every path I need to travel and closing doors I should not enter.

# Journey Through the Days

**July 5, 2010**

Looking back over the last few days, I see that the journey to this day was very interesting. There were two funerals in the family. I am also noticing ministries shifting due to wrong decisions they made. For example, marriage planning that should not happen. The Spirit of the Lord is revealing all these things and they are painful. Now I have to share the news, or should I say, share the revelations. Once again, I have to give revelations that are not favorable to man. "It is for God's glory and for their good." I keep telling myself. The love I have for God pushes me to move and let Him speak through me. I cannot ignore the words He gave me. I knew it would take courage to do it and I asked Him over and over to give it to me. I do not have a choice. I delivered the word. Whatever happens now is out of my hands. I have done what was assigned to me. I feel free. It is between them and God.

One thing I can say is that the journey to this day of liberty has cost me more than I would have been willing to pay alone. But I was paying it with God. Sacrifices, rejections, disappointments, and upsets are part of the journey with God. Obedience is better than sacrifice. I was obedient; now I will continue to do my Lord's will in and out of season.

Scriptures:

The Lord shall preserve your going out and your coming in from this time forth, and even forevermore. Psalm 121:8 (NKJV)

The heavens declare the glory of God and the firmament shows His handiwork. Psalm 19:1(NKJV)

Thank You, Lord, for revealing Your will to me and strengthening me to do it.

# A Night's Journey

**July 10, 2010**

This is about a dream. I woke up and when I went back to sleep, it continued where it left off. This was a dream that continued no matter how I tried to stop it. Without revealing the dream, I will give you the revelation I received from it.

I noticed the peace in a bad situation. I wanted to cry, scream, and give up but all I could do was believe that God was still in control and that I had His peace within me. Everyone looked at me and wondered when I was going to release something by yelling or screaming. God held me through it all. So think about the worst thing that could happen to you or something that already happened to you, that you did not have any control. Was your reaction calm or "raging"? Did you cry or just sit there numb? Warnings were placed in my path. I just did not know it at the time. But afterward, I knew in my heart it was going to happen. God sends us warnings. He prepares us for situations. We ignore them or just cannot understand them. I did scream at the end and woke up. I screamed because I realized the warning was there and I ignored it. A watchman is supposed to sound the alarm. Well, that was a journey which was uncomfortable all night and that morning, it kept playing in my mind. I did what I read in a book suggested. I went for a prayer walk. I looked at God's glory, the things and creatures He created; the trees, birds, insects, water, sky, and more. God is in control of the universe. He knows every creature and plant. He also knows what our future will be. Trust in Him, stay close to Him, and listen to His warning before it's too late.

## Scriptures:

The Lord is my light and my salvation, whom shall I fear? The Lord is the strength of my life; of whom shall I be afraid? Psalm 27:1(NKJV)

Now to Him who is able to keep you from stumbling, and to present you faultless before the presence of His glory with exceeding joy. Jude 24 (NKJV)

Thank You, Lord, for the Holy Spirit. He is the Spirit of Truth.

# A Night's Journey of Temptation

**July 18, 2010**

Looking at all my classmates gives me a feeling of joy. The laughter, smiles, conversations, and actions are so amazing. Getting to this place was not an easy journey. However, it was worth all the struggles. I am still praying that God will manifest Himself and touch someone's heart. Everything was in place, the food, drinks, and music were all in place. I was observing reactions to the place, food, and the music. Listening to the music was not a struggle for me. But when that certain song played, it brought back memories. Thank You, Lord, for strength. The temptations of past feelings for a certain person rose again. It was never a physical connection but a wanting connection. It was as if he knew it too. He kept getting in my space as if he trying to remind me of the attraction I had for him. I never believed he was attracted to me in school. Now, I need to pray for disconnection with him. I need to love him as a brother and as a child of the Most High God. I never told him how I felt in school but he seems to know it. I am not in school now I am a mature woman of God who lives by the Word and not by flesh.

The pressure to dance was getting hard to resist, not because I wanted to dance but to keep from saying "leave me alone" all night. I was very content talking to people and watching them dance. "But God," is all I can say. But God! One person did something that he was not fully aware of. He gave the DJ a gospel CD to play for me. He played two songs so I was revived in the midst of it all: "God is trying to tell you something" and "I know I've been changed". I stood up and praised God in that room. They joined me. For different reasons, I am sure of that. I know that most of them really believe Jesus is the Son of God and acknowledge Him as Lord.

Now I lay me down to sleep, I pray the Lord my soul He keeps. Forgive me for letting thoughts come in my mind and keep me strong all the time. Help me to disconnect from evil people and evil things. Keep me under Your merciful wings. Clean my heart from wrong connection. And Lord, help me to withstand pressure. Keep us safe until we meet again. Lord, watch over my dear, dear friends.

## Scriptures:

Oh, taste and see that the Lord is good; blessed is the man who trusts in Him! Psalms 34:8 (NKJV)

Blessed be the God and Father of our Lord Jesus Christ, who has blessed us with every spiritual blessing in heavenly places in Christ. Ephesians 1:3 (NKJV)

Thank You, Lord, for them. And thank you classmates for loving each other.

# A Reflection of a Journey

## July 24, 2010

It is early. The house is quiet. I hear the music playing in the background. The world seems still except for a few people walking their dogs. I wonder how many started with a prayer and a Word before focusing on the dogs. I begin to think about the recent captivity I experienced. Can you imagine knowing someone who has isolated herself from the real world? The isolation was not only in a physical sense but also in an emotional and mental one. No one can get in or get close. I noticed she was slowly dying due to no close or healthy relationships. Her eyes were focused on herself only. No matter how people try to reach out, she withdrew before getting too close. One reason is because one cannot break through the door. For someone to be captured in their own mind and an isolated emotion is very sad. No real joy. To describe it, I would say the whole thing is a pseudo life, pseudo emotions, pseudo love and pseudo joy. Every time someone gets close or try to get close, she finds a way to reject them. The truth is real but very bitter and, for lack of a better word, "ugly". It is ugly in this case, captured in a world where you just "exist"; often making excuses for that captivity. If only a way will be made to stir up the truth, things will change and joy will be there. Everything might fall apart including her spirit, emotions, schedule, and standards of doing things. I am wondering if freedom will come through death only. There is a level of isolation she has in the bedroom. Those empty rooms have darkness, darkness that comes from fear. The fear increases and the fear ensures that no one is welcome to keep isolation. Do not suggest a way out to freedom because she will run back into the cage (home) and stay until you have forgotten or given up. One way she finds comfort is to hold on to material things as pleasure because they do not die. They do not hurt others. She is holding on to the prison bars to stay safe from reality. She seems to get a high from others' misfortune. She covers it up by making a statement of concern after someone questions her sincerity. Her excitement comes from food, spending money on things, and talking about things she treasures; for example, the degrees, cars she owns, and how much money she earns. But none have given life instead it has given her a false life of pleasure and false security. She's willing to share or give only if she is getting something back. When you talk to her about your issues, she is busy thinking about herself. As soon as you finish, she goes back to her conversation about her. It is hard to break through the doors which she hides behind.

### Scripture:

My help comes from the Lord, Who made heaven and earth. Psalm 121:2 (NKJV)

Lord, help them. Show truth before it's too late. Open the doors of her heart and renew her mind.

# Journey of Seeking God for Answers

**August 1, 2010**

Watching a person in so much pain, young and full of life, but now so much pain it seems as if age had come and taken over before its time. As I think about the Word, by His stripes we are healed. That Word has played over and over in my head. I believe God, even though no healing has taken place yet. I know that everyone will not be healed on this side of heaven. Some will suffer a long time before they do. Some will die instantly. The Word says that the prayer of a righteous man prevails much. She prays, I pray, pastor prays, the family prays, but still, pain. I asked for answers because I want to offer hope. I offer strength to believe that God is still there. He is still there. He is still aware of the situation. Why God? Did they sin and this is the result? We all sin. Were they disobedient and You warned over and over but they refused to obey? Lord, I know You do not reveal everything to us. I am asking what is going on. Is there something that was not done or something that was done out of disobedience? Is it for Your glorification? Move God in every bone, move in every muscle. God give strength to bear the pains, to refuse the enemy's suggestion. Lord, give mercy and grace to Your child. Open eyes, open ears, open hearts to be close to You and to please You only. As I write this, I see disobedience Lord. We all have disobeyed. Lord, forgive please. Please give another chance to make it right. I wanted to help carry the burden, to carry the cross to the next step. I wanted to be there, to pray and pray, and cry out to God until something happen. God, now I understand. I pray for an obedient heart and a repentant heart. I pray that a U-turn will be done and go the right direction.

**Scriptures:**

Now faith is the substance of things hoped for, the evidence of things not seen. Hebrew 11:1 (NKJV)

Let not your heart be troubled; you believe in God, believe also in Me. John 14:1 (NKJV)

Lord, let Your will be done on earth as it is in heaven. Move and break the pride and fear which bound us. In Jesus' Name only, You can.

# Faith Journey

**August 8, 2010**

What a vision! I see a vision of "more than enough" to bless myself and others. The overflow of everything I need to do Your will. I stand on Your promise. I believe because the bills seem to come more, they are increasing. I believe in His outcome. Faith exist between the vision (promise) and the outcome. Faith is present to believe what seems to be impossible. Faith walks in every area of doubt, confusion, and unbelief. Faith is the key. Lord, I believe You when you said in Your word, You will never leave or forsake me and when You said You will supply all of my needs according to Your riches and glory. So Lord, I am still going to work in Your vineyard because faith without works is dead. I trust You and know it is already done. Thank You, Lord.

Faith is the key. We hear that a lot. We need to know we are on a faith journey. What does that mean? Its means to believe God and the Words in the Bible. No matter what is going on in life, believe that God will protect us. He will work everything out for our good if we love Him. We have to believe in our hearts. That means not to worry about the situations or the outcome. But know that God is in control no matter what the outcome will be. When it looks hopeless, things are still in God's control. Just keep seeking Him and be faithful to Him and His works.

### Scripture:

Let your light so shine before men, that they may see your good works and glorify your Father in heaven. Matthew 5:16 (NKJV)

Thank You, Lord, for giving us a measure of faith. Thank You for reassuring us that You will supply our needs.

# A Morning's Journey

**August 13, 2010**

Rising early and trying to make it to work. Just praying and focusing on God as I drive.

I noticed I was on the wrong road. After I realized it was the wrong road, I continued to drive hoping I would another road to get where I needed to be. I drove faster to make up for time I lost. But it was a dead end. There are nice houses on this road. Woods were all around here too. I turned around and started the journey to get back on the right track. It sounds like the definition of repentance.

We sometimes do the same on this journey of life. We make mistakes and get on the wrong road or path. We sometimes feel it is wrong but we keep going until we are sure. Prayerfully, we realize it soon and turn around and get on the right road. The wrong road might feel a little strange but we keep going because we see things which are nice, helpful, beautiful, interesting and more. We even see signs which make us think we are headed the right way but the whole time we are going the wrong way. I was a little nervous while driving on the dead end road; nervous about what I might see or when can I turn around. In life, we are nervous of what we might see, or when, or if we need to turn away.

I got back on the right road. I got to work two minutes late. I got delayed but made it safely. I made it to this point full of joy, peace, and laughter. In life, I can make it full of joy, peace, and laughter. I was so full of joy that I am excited about tomorrow. I am excited about each day with the Lord and being used by Him to glorify His Name. We have to stay on the right path. If we find ourselves off the right path, we need to turn around (repent) and get back on the right path. Blessings are waiting for us on the right path.

## Scriptures:

Blessed are those who hunger and thirst for righteousness, for they shall be filled. Matthew 5:6 (NKJV)

But seek first the kingdom of God and His righteousness, and all these things shall be added to you. Matthew 6:33 (NKJV)

God knows the plans He has for our lives. He has a plan of peace and not evil. Thank You, Lord.

# A Flight Journey

**August 16, 2010**

I am on a plane heading to Denver. I see how beautiful the clouds are while we fly above them. I like a bed of white fluffy cotton. I am reminded how awesome God is. He created this universe and He did it by speaking it into existence.

Just sitting here, I see a vision with a revelation. "You have to make it happen." It was dropped in my spirit. I must go and get my certification in counseling. I am so excited now. I have my directions. It was there the whole time but being up here made me more in tune with God this morning. God created the earth and I can see the earth from the plane. Looking down at it, I am very amazed. He created it and gave us dominion over it. We have to use the resources provided by Him. Thank You, Jesus. He already worked it out for us. We have to take steps and utilize the resources. Father, take care of us and give us favor. Most of all make our pathway straight. Thank You, Amen.

We need to keep moving forward and seek directions from Him. God planned our lives before we were born.

## Scripture:

Ask and it will be given to you; seek and you will find; knock and it will be opened to you. Matthew 7:7 (NKJV)

Lord, You keep this plane in the air. You are guiding us through it all. Thank You for protection.

# Reminiscence Journey

**August 17, 2010**

Once again, I am in the corporate world. I thought I wanted it. However, I still feel like something is missing. God allowed me to be in this environment because I wanted it so much. Now I am here again, I feel out of place. I do not get any fulfillment in it; people talking about themselves, throwing names out to be important, and sitting in a room where the majority of the participants are of the opposite sex. We are a very small portion of it. Why do we want to be part of that world? Is it because we are forbidden? We want what we do not need and what has been denied from us.

Now I want what God has for me. It was pulling on my desires to be part of a corporation. Now I am pleased with the area God has lead me to do. I am a woman of God. I have been called to do His will. I have been called to live a life of worshipping, teaching, and obeying God. It is good for some people but God did not have this path for me at this time of my life.

I get up and go where He tells me. I do not have an (earthly) boss or supervisor. There are others who are living this kind of life. I am wonderfully made to honor Him. Thank You, God, for setting my path before me. Lead me and guide me down the right path. The steps of a good "man" are order by God. Order my steps Heavenly Father. Glorify Yourself.

He is faithful enough to do what He promises. He loves enough to let us make choices. He is powerful enough to protect us. Please stay connected to the Father and find your purpose. It is fine, if your purpose is different from your peers. God created each of us unique.

**Scripture:**

And of His fullness we have all received, and grace for grace. John 1:16 (NKJV)

Lord, please continue to keep us on Your path.

# He's There for You

**August 19, 2010**

He's the God of this universe
He created all things
He knows every plant and creature
He created you to worship and praise Him
He knows you
When you are sad, ask Him to give you joy
When you are fearful ask Him for courage
When you are uncertain ask Him for direction
He knows the answers for all your questions
Let Him use you to glorify Himself
Believe Him, Trust Him, Follow Him
He is here for you
He is there for you
He is here with you
He is there with you

(I WROTE THIS FOR A 7 YEAR-OLD GIRL I MET IN DENVER. SHE WAS THERE FOR HER FATHER'S FUNERAL.)

I did not have an opportunity to give it to her but I pray that she knows God as her father.

**Scripture:**

Oh, come let us sing for joy to the Lord! Let us shout joyfully to the Rock of our salvation. Psalm 95:1 (NKJV)

# The ALL-Most Journey

**August 26, 2010**

The title comes from a message a pastor preached in Denver. I do not want to preach his message but I was getting revelations while he was speaking.

I was in class thinking about this trip. We had one more day left on the trip. I met people of different ethnicities, cultures, values, some anointed, some intimidated, and some uncertainties.

I was in a car accident; it was a little painful. It showed me once again how God is still in control, even though, He allowed this to happen to us. Celebrating at the Potter's House was a revival for me. The prophecies and the revelations were for me to hear from God again. Thank You, Lord, for providing while I am here. In the second class, we discussed how different people are and how we all are alike. God created us all. We are created by the same God. He created us to worship and praise Him. We have different ministries. He called some to teach, some to preach, some apostles, some to prophesy, and some helpers. He has given us a measure of faith. Our level of faith is different. The uniqueness of each person is there to glorify God. After all the opinions and remarks, it all boils down to knowing Who you belong to and why you are here. What is the purpose of me being alive? Am I living for myself or for my Maker? And after the Word last night I am in the right place. I feel I am about to see more promises come to past. I cannot explain it but I have to keep moving forward and rest in the Lord while He is leading me to the place I suppose to go. I know this is not a physical place but I am traveling on a path. A "prosperous" travel needs to be done with faith through trials, tribulation and blessings by the Holy Spirit. I can learn to get closer to Him as I move. I can also drop off things I do not need while I am going. Renew my mind to that level, Lord. Let the divine connections take place.

## Scriptures:

O Lord, How manifold are Your works! In wisdom You have made them all; the earth is full of Your possessions. Psalm 104:24 (NKJV)

The fear of the Lord is the beginning of wisdom; a good understanding have all those who do His commandments. Psalm 111:10 (NKJV)

Thank You, Lord, for the Word this week. Thank You for visions and revelations.

# A Journey of Self-Centeredness

**September 5, 2010**

I know I have to write something but I'm not sure what it is now. I feel empty inside. I am searching for Him. I pray for God to fill me with His Spirit. I ask for forgiveness of my sins. I tried to name them so confession will take place and I can be forgiven. In I John 1:9, its states, "Confess your sins and He is faithful and just to forgive and cleanse from all unrighteousness". So I am confessing my sins. I remember feeling like this once before when He was cleansing me. I asked Him to purify me and I went through the purification stage. The more He purifies me the more I look like Him. More of His characteristics are in me. More of the Fruit of the Spirit is within me.

Since the accident in Denver, I have been trying to get the appropriate people to handle the bills. I will admit that it is a challenge but God will take care of it. God, I know You are still in charge of me. As soon as I got home my dad got sick. I had to take a week from work to ensure he is taken care of. He is in the nursing home by his request. He talks as if he wants to stay forever. I am trying to rest between errands for him. I do not mind. He needs to be taken care of and I am able to do my part and beyond by God's grace. I love my dad and he needs me now, I want to be there always to help him. He was there for me when I needed him.

God, God, God, I just need to call You. Now I know why I have to write. I have to acknowledge that I am a little self-centered now. I am feeling a little down and there is no one to talk with. Everyone I associate with is having problems themselves. So once again, Father, it is You and I. I need a break-through. I need reviving, restoring, and reconnecting. Come Holy Spirit and fill me. Come and comfort me, the Comforter. I still have joy. Thank You, God, for listening again. Only You can do it. Thanks for coming right away.

Heal my body, heal my emotions, and heal my spirit.

**SCRIPTURES:**

You will keep him in perfect peace, whose mind is stayed on You, because he trusts in You. Isaiah 26:3 (NKJV)

The Lord is my Shepherd; I shall not be want. Psalm 23:1 (NKJV)

And we know that all things work together for good to those who love God, to those who are called according to His purpose. Romans 8:28 (NKJV)

Only, You can. Incline Your ears once again.

# Morning Journey

**September 12, 2010**

I got up and looked out the door. While standing on the balcony, I noticed the residue from the rain last night. There was thunder, rain, lighting, and wind. I remember the song, "Like the Dew in the Morning"; the dew was heavy this morning. Can you imagine God's Spirit falling on you that thick? The rain was used for a spiritual look. The storm came last night. But it is gone this morning. Joy comes in the morning. The rain was soaked up by many trees, flowers, and grass. They will use it to grow and to get strength. We should use the storm in our lives to get stronger, to grow closer and larger in Christ. I saw some flowers drown by the rain. Some of us let our storm in our lives drown us in fear, sorrow, etc. The wind blows some of the dead leaves from the trees. We should ask God to deliver us from dead things (sins) in our lives while we are going through. If I have to go through this storm, please take away things that do not give You glory. Take away my idols, faults, sin, etc. Thank You, Lord. Puddles in the road are evident of the rain and storm. I noticed a car drove through the puddle with no problem. We should keep going and moving forward through the storm. After it's over, we should just keep going and giving God praise. Some go around puddles. We sometimes try to find ways to get around trials and tribulations. We will have trials but some are not meant for us to go through. They are traps from the enemy. So be mindful of what the Spirit is saying and He will steer us away from some of those traps. He will guide us and show us truth. Take the left if He says go left; stop if He says stop. He knows a puddle is there which will stop your engine.

God can use our storms to glorify Him. He can use it to change our relationship with Him. He can use them to change our way of thinking. And He can use it to increase our faith. Thank God for being there through the storm. Our storms give us more of Him to grow and get stronger likes the trees and grass.

## SCRIPTURES:

You will show me the path of life; in Your presence is fullness of joy; at your right hand are pleasures forevermore. Psalm 16:11 (NKJV)

As for God, His way is perfect; the word of the Lord is proven. He is a shield for all who trust in Him. II Samuel 22:31 (NKJV)

Thank You, Lord, for Your Peace.

# Journey of Seeking

**September 15, 2010**

I am in training for the corporate world. I cannot focus on this one for some reason. I do not know why I am feeling out of place again. Most of the time when I am in these corporate meetings, I feel out of place.

I have been looking around to see if anyone else seems to be out of place. I have to calm down and let God do His work through me and/or to me. Just go, just say, just do as normal. That same feeling has hit me again when I sit in the classroom. "Why, why am I here to this training?" Well, let God do it. Last night in the hotel, I could do nothing but pray all night. I was thanking God and asking Him to cleanse me. I love to seek God before my day starts. Lord, I am so hungry for You. Move on Your people the only way You can. A peace and an expectation has come over me. In Your time, Lord, at Your appointed place.

I must have patience and wait on the Lord. Watch and see His glory.

**Scripture:**

When the Day of Pentecost had fully come, they were all with one accord in one place. Acts 2:1 (NKJV)

Thank You, Lord for moving during their plans and programs.

# Protection on the Journey

**October 9, 2010**

I had a dream that the Hand of God was protecting and intervening in our lives. The dream was about a young lady trying to get back into a situation she had been delivered from years. Why was she trying to do it? The enemy was trying to take her backward and she was allowing it. But God kept putting people on her path to minister to her so her mind could be on doing His will. He intervened by sending others with a need so she could forget about herself. He sent a woman who needed prayer. He sent a nephew who needed guidance. No matter who God sent, she still insisted on doing wrong. Even though the plans did not come together, she went anyway. When she got there the person was gone. All the glory goes to God for the delay. He protected her even when she did not want His protection. This was a dream but a message for many of us.

God knows we can get ourselves in some trouble. Often His Spirit tries to tell us. He sometimes puts us late or early or redirects our path. However, some of us try so hard to do wrong that we insist on going to the "trouble". When we make choices to ignore the Protector and Intercessor, we have to deal with the results.

The Holy Spirit will do His job. He is the Spirit of Truth. We do not have to understand what He is doing but we need to trust the truth.

## Scriptures:

Shout joyfully to the Lord, all the earth; break forth in song, rejoice and sing praises. Psalm 98:4 (NKJV)

Commit your way to the Lord; Psalm 37:5a (NKJV)

Lord, please continue to let Your Spirit guide us.

# A Guide for the Journey

**October 9, 2010**

I know God chose me for a service (ministry). Sometimes I wonder if I am on the right path. I guess it's because it seems as if it is not moving forward. So, I have been praying to God to guide me to the right path. I have been reading what He told me when I got ordained and when I first got into ministry. Those words are playing in my head often lately. Sometimes we get very impatient and get into things that are not good. This morning I read Jeremiah chapter 1. I got a revelation from God. I am unique but anointed and ordained by God. Jeremiah 1:10 says, "There is a time to pull down, destroy, root up and there is a time to build and plant". I will go and speak whatever He commands me to do or say. They might not like it but they will know that He was in the place. Do not be afraid of the leaders of the land. God will protect me and hide me under His wings. However, it is better to suffer for His Kingdom then for evil. (I Peter) They have forsaken God, worshipped idols, gods, car, people, ministry, etc. God wants His word to be told. Whether it is that He loves them or His is warning them, He wants them to know. So we need to pull down the enemy's camp and uproot things which are holding God's people down. We need to destroy all existing bondages by using the Power of God. We need to build up His kingdom, build up His temples, and plant His seed (Word) in the hearts of His people. The captive need to be set free and the broken hearts healed. Go where He sends you, open your mouth, prepare yourself, arise and do not be dismayed before their faces. Be of good courage.

We have the Power in us to make miracles happen. We can lay hands on the sick and God will heal them through us. We need to stop focusing on material things so much and focus on the will of God. Our motto should be, "Put God first".

**SCRIPTURES:**

O Lord, our Lord. How excellent is Your Name in all the earth! Psalm 8:9 (NKJV)

The Lord shall preserve your going out and your coming in from this time forth and even forevermore. Psalm 121:8 (NKJV)

Lord, You are the First and the Last.

# A Journey Back

**October 30, 2010**

A client explained something to me a few days ago. He was talking how important it is being in people lives. He also talked about how it seems as if young people are rejected today. I was telling him that things were different for me for about a couple of month. How I felt different I would not go into great details about but he understood. He said I lost focus and we all do that from time to time. That hit my spirit in a mighty way. That is why now I see again, I know again, I hear again. Somewhere I lost focus on the purpose and on the direction, He is taking me. I believe I began focusing on making a living and to provide monies for bills. I lost focus on Who provide the money for bills and Who works it all out for me. I was trying to do what would be logical. "Ha"

I know he was right because I was just telling myself a day before that I felt complete again. I see people's issues; I see their struggles and hear their pains in their voices. I hear it and God sends me again with a Word or just a smile. I must keep focus because others are affected by it. God has work for us all to do. There is no little work or big work in the Kingdom. There is work to do so obey God and do it willingly. Whatever He calls each of us to do, that is what we need stay focused on. Stay focused on Him and the path you are supposed to be traveling on even if you do not understand that path. "Blind Faith" (TRUST)

I heard it called that a long time ago. Have faith in Him without knowing or understanding everything. Just believe that He has your best interest and is taking care of you like no one else can. Ask Abram and Moses. They did not know everything God was doing but they trusted that He was in control of their endings. Believe that He is God and that He created you.

**Scriptures:**

May the Lord answer you in the day of trouble; May the name of the God of Jacob defend you. Psalm 20:1 (NKJV)

The Lord is my light and my salvation; whom shall I fear? The Lord is the strength of my life; of whom shall I be afraid? Psalm 27:1 (NKJV)

Thank You, Lord, for keeping me.

# Journey to the Promise

**October 30, 2010**

This title will be used more than once. God promised me so much. Sometimes on these journeys, a shift will occur. I recognize a shift with this promise: "More than enough". I remember a few years ago, it was placed in my spirit. I found out that I could ask Him for more. I could have the abundant life that is promised to us. I can have it now. I can ask Him to give me enough for me and for others. I can ask Him to let me live comfortably and lack for nothing. I do not have to lack in the Spirit or in material things. I declare good health, good relationships, good financial status, and good works that whatever I do will be pleasing to Him. I will have more than enough so I can bless others. I am working in "more than enough"; it is about to manifest here on earth. The earth belongs to Him and everything in it and I will get what He promised me. The Spirit of believing is upon me. I can stop seeking help to pay bills, to buy things I need. I can help others and pray for their goods. I can pray for liberty to set them free from the enemy's hands. I can pray for a forgiving spirit upon them. I can pray to guide them to the path of righteousness through Jesus Christ. I will be free to do His work from city to city.

God thanks for the abundance of provisions. You are my provision. I got it. Thank You, Lord!

Whatever I ask in Your Name....
Jesus is Lord and Savior
He is above everyone
He died for us
He lived for us
He rose for us
He did it for us
He is coming back for us

Live for Him, wait on Him, work for Him, your life style is your worship.

**Scriptures:**

One thing I desired of the Lord, that will I seek; that I may dwell in the house of the Lord all the days of my life. Psalm 27:4 (NKJV)

Oh, taste and see that the Lord is good; blessed is the man who trusts in Him. Psalm 34:8 (NKJV)

I no longer live but Christ lives in me. Thank You, Lord.

# Journey to My Promise

**November 9, 2010**

When I was on my way to Albany, I heard a CD where the speaker was talking about visions. The Spirit came upon me and I began praising God. I felt His Spirit move within me. And I began to declare in Jesus' Name and asking God for His promise and protection. Others came into mind as I prayed in the Spirit. I was once again amazed at the Power of God. All I could think was, "I am ready in Your Name". I am willing and available. Strengthen me and the others who want to be used by You to work in Your Kingdom. It is already done. It is time to get in the purpose that He calls us to. It is time to get in place. To be in the purpose God called for you means to be in the proper place and the holy place. The land of milk and honey is in His purpose for your life.

God is not a man so He cannot lie. Whatever He promises will be fulfilled. This journey is a trust journey. We should trust God and walk by faith no matter what it looks like. Believe the promises.

**Scripture:**

He has made everything beautiful in its time. Ecclesiastes 3:11a (NKJV)

Thank You, Lord, for getting me out of the sinful world and into Your family.

# A Journey in My Dream

**November 16, 2010**

I had an odd dream. First, I was at church and my cousin was preaching. While he was preaching, his wife stood up and starts preaching. When I got ready to leave I saw a member of a local church and we began to talk. As I was walking away, he was commenting something not pleasant about me, "for a married man". So I left him. I was at another place in the dream and another man was there trying to talk with me. I let him know that I was not interested in dating but he kept trying to get me to go out with him. I left.

I shifted to another place in the dream. I was with my classmates, even the ones who were dead. No one wanted to talk with me because I wanted to talk about God. We stopped by my cousin's (who is also a classmate) job. I thought we were going to talk about the Lord because we always do but she only talked with them and not me. After leaving her job, we made it to a house where there was a large yellow and white snake. I ran out the house. Every time I would go inside they would release him and I would leave out again. They followed me everywhere with that snake. I fought and ran. I decided to get far away from them.

Now this is the weird part in the dream. A lady wanted me to deliver the snake on a truck. I remember feeling afraid, nervous, and as if it was a setup. But I did it anyway. The snake got out of the truck. I could not get out because I was afraid to move. After a while, I got out anyway through the fear. I realized a lust spirit came upon me while I was with my classmate. I did not tell him. A girl (I don't know) walked with me and said the lust feeling was upon her also. I guess she was in the house. She had discernment too. I kept fighting the lust feeling and by the grace of God, I overcame it.

At the end of the dream, one of the guys came to me and laid before me in a seductive way. I pressed my nails in his thigh and he left. I could also feel me pressing pain on him in the dream. So much of the dream seems to be real to me. When I woke up, I kept seeing the snake throughout the day and it was on one of my client's face. I remember last week feeling uneasy about the way he looked at me. This dream might have had something to do with him.

**Scriptures:**

Finally, my brethren, be strong in the Lord and in the power of His might. Ephesians 6:10 (NKJV)

Rejoice in the Lord always. Again, I will say it again, rejoice! Philippians 4:4 (NKJV)

Lord, hide me under Your wing. You are my shield. I pray for Your protection and guidance.

# A Reflection of the Journey in a Dream

**November 17, 2010**

I began to reflect on the dream again. You know what? The enemy is all around! He is trying to be a part of everything that a child of God is doing. Why? Because he wants to destroy the works of the saints and he wants to keep us in a state of confusion. He also wants to keep the anointing Power from delivering, healing, directing, encouraging, or setting God's people free. We need to be watchful (mindful) of our path, behavior, attitudes, and daily living. If a gap or gate is open, that joker (devil) will try to get in to destroy anything he could destroy. The enemy will use others to assist him. That is why the "friends" were trying to bring him (the snake) to me. They wanted me to drive him around with me in the dream. He got out of the truck because of the anointing on me. We cannot compromise. I know now after reading the books of Jeremiah and Galatians, it is okay to be an outsider. I might be talked about but I have to do God's will. I should be God's mouth piece here on earth. Paul said, "Men did not teach me but it was the revelation of Jesus Christ". I can say the same thing. God revealed some of Paul and Jeremiah's gifts in me. Some of my journeys are similar to theirs. I must give glory to God through pain, persecution, rejection, victories, sorrows, and much more.

Glory to God! Glory to God! The True Living God is worthy to be praised. I am a child of God. He is my provision, my King, my Master, my Savior, my Friend, and my Redeemer. He is the Great I Am. Lord, strengthen me to do the assignments, tasks, whatever You call me to do. Lead me, show me, and guide me. I am Your child. Send me.

Like in the dream, we cannot fear the enemy. God did not give me a spirit of fear but Power, love and sound mind. Another interesting thing about the snake was the color. The colors were beautiful. We have to understand the enemy is not an ugly, scary thing. He will make himself appear in a way that you will not be frightened, so ask God for discernment.

**Scriptures:**

My help comes from the Lord, Who made heaven and earth. Psalm 121:2 (NKJV)

Now faith is the substance of things hoped for, the evidence of things not seen. Hebrews 11:1 (NKJV)

The Lord is blessing us right now and always. We need to give Him praise.

# A Journey with Others

**November 19, 2010**

I am back into a familiar environment. A class with others learning and socializing. I noticed we have different people from different areas and offices. However, it was strange not to feel any culture or subculture differences.

This is the first time in a setting of training that I feel no separation or bias attitudes. Everyone seems to be on the same level. Now this is how children of God should act. We must know that we are special and wonderfully made. We can be assured that God loves us all. He will provide for us all. He looks at us and sees His Son's blood if we are saved. And He pours out His blessing of grace and mercy. No one is trying to act more important than the other. No one is blowing their own horn when they introduce themselves.

We have to stop thinking we are so important that others should feel lower than us. We all have what we have by the grace of God. We accomplished what we accomplished by the grace of God. If we think about it, we are in the same boat. We all are going through struggles, trials, tribulations, ups and downs.

The training was great!

**Scriptures:**

Let not let your heart be troubled; you believe in God, believe also in Me. John 14:1 (NKJV)

Let your light so shine before men, that they may see your good works and glorify your Father in heaven. Matthew 5:16 (NKJV)

Thank You, Lord, for keeping us safe as we travel from state to state.

# JOURNEY AT THE AIRPORT

November 29, 2010

I arrived early to ensure I can handle any problems before the flight. Thank God it all went okay. The process of flying is the barrier. I heard a passenger say something almost like that earlier. I said to myself, "She is right". When parking your car, you have to follow the signs then when the sign cannot help you any longer, one need to find a person. I finally parked; then the shuttle left before I got out of the car. I had to look for another shuttle and there was one parked at the end of the row. I began walking toward it and they told me to go back to my car so they can pick me up. I started back then they called me back to the van. Okay people! The weather was cold and damp. Everyone who knows me knows that I was not pleased. I remained calm and refused to get frustrated at the time. The van stopped at the south gate. Everyone got off except me. I asked about going to the North gate. She took me without any hassle or negative remarks. This part of the process was easier than ever before; that is a miracle alone. I got through the check-in with no problems. I got another miracle in this part of the process. I got through security with no additional problems other than the normal hassles of taking off shoes, jackets and putting everything in bins. I felt sorry for people with children. I watched a family in line who had lots of packages, bags, and children to handle. One of their children was crying because he wanted his toy. He did not want it on the security belt. We should to react in a Christian matter when things are uncomfortable. We cannot or should not act like the babies.

The employees are not friendly. I know they have a job to do but what happened to speaking to the customers. Good customer services begin with a smile and a greeting. Customers are very important to every business. Even when we are doing our jobs, we need to show love to others. We are ministering on our vocational jobs.

Now I am at the gate two hours early. I am people watching. If I could use one word to give you a picture of the people, it would be "unhappy". You should try it sometimes at a mall or at a park. No one seems to be happy to go to their destinations. I expect frustration from single mothers who had to balance bags and children. I also expect frustration from a person going on to a funeral. But I see the faces of couples, families, and multiple parties looking as if they lost their best friend. I would think they would be having a "ball" traveling together.

Employees are buzzing about the Christmas party. I see excitement when they talk about it but not any excitement toward the customers. They forgot the customer service this morning.

I notice different languages, different skin color, and different social groups, but they seem to have two things in common: they are human beings and unhappy human beings. I could be just for the moment of getting through this process of trying to get from point "A" to point "B" and maybe to point "C". It could be a hassle at the airport.

As we try to get from glory to glory and from level to level, we should know that we are being watched by God and others. Are others seeing the glory of God in our struggles, our transformations, our valleys and our mountains? Do they see "unhappy" lives? Are we just trying to get to point "A" to point "B" to point "C"? These are questions we need to answer and examine ourselves. We have to take this Christian journey so let's make the best of it and get stronger from it. There may be a little trouble, a little hassle, or a little delay but it is worth the trouble to go all the way. The reward is greater than the journey. Trust God to take every step with you. Smile, love, be of good cheer and make others' day a little joyous.

**On the plane:**

People are talking, laughing, smiling, and greeting each other. It had to be the process of getting to this point making them so unhappy. Some of the same people I saw in the airport are on the plane talking with strangers and laughing. They seem to let go of the struggle after they got on the plane. I guess they feel relieve and comfortable now.

The process is not always pleasant, but we can ask God to order our steps (process).

## Scriptures:

Blessed are those who hunger and thirst for righteousness for they will be filled. Matthew 5:6 (NKJV)

But seek first the kingdom of God and His righteousness, and all these things shall be added to you. Matthew 6:33 (NKJV)

Therefore, whatever you want men to do to you, do also to them, for this is the Law and the Prophets. Matthew 7:12 (NKJV)

Set your mind on things above, not on things on the earth. Colossians 3:2 (NKJV)

Make a joyful shout to the Lord, all you lands. Psalm 100:1 (NKJV)

I feel that traveling means to move from one place to another. Thank You, Lord, for traveling with us. Let Your Word be a lamp to my feet and a light to my path. (Psalm 119:105)

# JOURNEY THROUGH THE SKIES

November 29, 2010

Above the clouds, I see a bright light. It looks like a reflection from the sun. The clouds look like cotton. They look so soft and plush. The blue sky above me is so beautiful. God is so wonderful. He created all this and gave man the ability to fly in the sky. In addition to the glory of seeing His work, I have found a gospel praise channel on the plane radio system.

The song playing now is, "It's gonna be alright". I thank God for the song of encouragement. God, I want to spend time with You on this trip. I want to hear Your voice. I want to go into worship with You. Thank You, for what You are putting in place now.

I am excited about the time alone. I will get a chance to meditate on the Word and think about where I came from and how far God has brought me. It has been a journey. But look how far I have come from the little girl who was so insecure and from the young adult who wanted to be accepted. Now, I am a woman of the True Living God who loves life, loves God, loves doing His work and loves His people. God is so close to us. When I am in the air, I looked up and see if I could see Him or an angel up there. It might sound crazy but I feel ever so close to Him in the air. I know it is not the geography location but our hearts.

SCRIPTURES:

Oh, give thanks to the Lord, for He is good! For His mercy endures forever. Psalm 118:1 (NKJV)

Forever, O Lord, Your word is settled in heaven. Your faithfulness endures to all generations; You established the earth and it abides. Psalm 119: 89-90 (NKJV)

Thank You, Lord, for bringing me through the doubts and insecurities.

# Journey to the Unknown

**November 30, 2010**

Searching for a connection but to what or whom? Feeling something is missing. I feel like something is happening. I am here for training for the new position I have now. But I feel I am here for a new position in the ministry. I want to be in total obedience to the move of God. Here in another training session but in body only. It is hard to listen and focus on this training. I know You have ordained this time. You have planned this move. Help me to listen for Your voice; help me to know when You are moving. Stay focused on the invisible world along with the visible world.

Stay focused on who I am. Prayer is needed for the sick. Do not let me miss the opportunities You set before me on this trip. Open my eyes and ears to You only. Thank You for being in control. The steps of a good person are ordered by You. Order my steps. I heard it from the instructor. I do not know if anyone else heard it but I did. Wow! It was so clear. Thank You, Lord.

The instructor was teaching and it seems as if he was talking to me about ministry. It was very strange. This is an odd trip. All the information in the classes are not getting to me on the vocation level but on a spiritual level.

I see the mountains and how beautiful they are from a distance. God made them. It is awesome how the plants know which climate to grow in. The plants in Georgia might not survive here in Colorado and vice versa. It is awesome how our body can heal itself if we take care of it. God created it all.

**Scriptures:**

O Lord, how manifold are Your works! Psalm 104:24a (NKJV)

I will sing to the Lord as long as I live; I will sing praise to my God while I have my being. Psalm 104:33 (NKJV)

Thank You, for the guidance and for already putting my life in Your hand.

# Journey to the Truth

**December 1, 2010**

I am still in training in Denver. I woke up talking to God about truth. Lots of ideas and information we are getting does not line up with God's truth. We can read the Word and still not understand the truth. We have to ask God to show us Truth and teach us His Truth. I am seeking God to love Him with all my soul, mind, and strength. I am also making a decree to seek His Truth.

I found a label on the tea bags I used this morning. I pray for truth often because I want God's Truth to rule over my life. "We know truth not only by reason but also by heart", was Blaise Pascal's message on the label. When I got up, I asked God to put His armor on me. One part is to gird my loins (waist) with truth. We need to stand in truth, to live by truth, to know when truth is present and know when truth is present. We need discernment. Let truth be within my soul. We need to walk in truth and live by the truth of God. I asked God to reveal truth in all situations. My prayer is that truth is revealed and His will be done and that He gets the glory.

**Scriptures:**

The fear of the Lord is the beginning of wisdom; a good understanding have all those who do His commandments. His praise endures forever. Psalm 111:10 (NKJV)

And the Word became flesh and dwelt among us and we beheld His glory, the glory of the only begotten of the Father, full of grace and truth. John 1:14 (NKJV)

Thank You, Lord, for Your truth. Thank You for grace.

# Another Day's Journey

**December 2, 2010**

That is a song; "It's another's day journey and I'm glad about it." I thank You, Lord, for Your new mercy this morning. I thank You, for Your Spirit. I want to be in Your presence. I know You ordained this time and place for me this week. You plan is for me to be here in Denver and make divine connections. Have Your way, Lord. Open my eyes, ears and heart to see, hear, and know what the Spirit is revealing to me. This is the day of breakthrough. Move Lord; order my steps. Move in this place. Thank You for provisions and for making a way out of no way. God, I am excited about Your glory. Teach me, lead me, hold me, and protect me. Reveal truth to me and let Your will be done and glorify Yourself.

Thanks for the truth last night. Thanks for giving my eyes to the truth about bonding. I love You, Lord. Forgive me this day. We are all here to encourage each other. We are to pray with each other and to pray for each other. If we bind together, two or three of us, we can declare and proclaim the Power of God. We can proclaim His Word and His works. We have the Power of God and the authority of God to win, to achieve, and to prosper.

It is another day's journey and I am glad about it! You gave me eyes to see and I am very thankful about it. You gave me food to eat and a shelter over my head and I am very, very, thankful about it.

**Scripture:**

You will keep him in perfect peace, whose mind is stayed on You, because he trusts in You. Trust in the Lord forever, for in Yah, the Lord is everlasting strength. Isaiah 26:3-4 (NKJV)

Thank You, Lord, for teaching us to love one another.

# Journey Home

**December 5, 2010**

I was reflecting on the journey from Denver to home. Sometimes we don't know what God did after we finish a task or assignment. We don't know sometimes exactly what He did when we went through a revival. But we know He did something and He moved in a way we cannot explain. God did that again on this assignment. He moved in such a way that I cannot explain. All I can say is that truth was revealed and there was a disconnection from bondage through that truth. He made divine connection; He put His plan in motion to manifest the truth. He did what He does best: loves us, provides for us, heals us, delivers us, and glorified Himself.

On the plane, it was like a renewing of my spirit. He fixed it so I was the only one sitting on that row. I just started to praise Him for His goodness. I cannot explain a specific thing but I know in my spirit that God fixes the whole person. He did something and was continuing in the process. He worked on me physically, emotionally, spiritually and mentally. He also worked in my relationships. We have to be able to handle the blessing so He is preparing us through all those avenues. He does not want us to lack in anything. We have to go when He says go (physical journey); we have to let go of things and people when He tells us to (emotionally journey); we have to let Him dwell within us in a way our spirits connect and He will guide us through our spirit (spiritual journey). We have to think without the stinky thinking we used to have before we had a close relationship with Him. I did not say before we accepted Jesus. We still had stinky thinking then but when His Spirit washed us, our thinking should change. Our minds should be changed to a new man (mental journey). We have to be so close to Him that He is more important than our mother, father, sister, brother, child, spouse, degrees, and etc. We have to be so close to Him. We should feel that we could die and would die if He rejected us. We need to feel that we will not be whole if He leaves us. We should feel that we cannot go a day without talking with

Him (relationship). I felt His Spirit moving within me on that plane. I felt His presence within my soul. He is worthy to be acknowledged, praised, honored, worshipped and to be the "first" in your life. He fills the void within you that no one can fill. He will set the plan and direct it. Just wait and listen for Him to "speak". I knew a change had been done on the inside of me a long time ago because I live differently. I think differently and talk differently. Now He was doing a change inside I could not explain. I will say that I walk differently, not so much in the physical but each step feels as if I was walking in authority. I have an assurance that I am called for a purpose; I have been chosen for such a time as this to do a work that is ordained by God. I thought I could see before when I got ordained but now I can see more clearly.

## SCRIPTURES:

Have I not commended you? Be strong and of courage. Do not be afraid, nor be dismayed, for the Lord your God is with you wherever you go. Joshua 1:9 (NKJV)

If you abide in Me, and My words abide in you, you will ask what you desire, and it shall be done for you. By this My Father is glorified, that you bear much fruit; so you will be My disciples. John 15:7-8 (NKJV)

And he who does not take his cross and follow after Me is not worthy of Me. He who finds his life will lose it, and he who loses his life for My sake will find it. Matthew 10:38-39 (NKJV)

All the thanks go to God, our Lord, our Savior. Glorify Yourself.

# A Journey to My Purpose

**December 8, 2010**

I am away from home again. The purpose has been released. I feel it in the atmosphere. You might not fully understand but as you get closer to God you will understand. Sometimes you might know and sometimes you might not know what is going on with you. Remember in all your getting, get understanding from Him. I am reminded over and over daily of Your purpose. You see God's hands moving around you everywhere you go. Stay focused on Him and let Him have His way. The promise, the vision is coming forth. It will manifest very, very soon on earth.

A change has taken place within me, within my mind mostly. God has touched me in a way that is hard to explain. Faith is a very important part of your purpose. An increase of faith is very important to reach your purpose. Why? The answer is because you have to trust Him when you do not have a clue. You have to believe that He knows what the plan is and He will make the plan come to reality to us. Get a hungry love for God because He is God, not because of things or stuff but because His love will keep you. He will touch you in such a way that you will want to be in His presence daily. No one or nothing can take His place.

If you feel empty, ask Him to fill you. If you feel as if you do not belong anywhere, ask God to direct you to His purpose for your life.

### Scripture:

As for God, His way is perfect; the word of the Lord is proven; He is a shield to all who trust in Him. II Samuel 22:31 (NKJV)

Hide us, Lord, under Your wing. Open doors we supposed to go through and close the ones we are not supposed to go through.

# Taking a Journey in Trust

**December 11, 2010**

Today is the day for a praise service. One might ask "why" this service is so different. The Spirit of God has shown me that this is more than just a praise service. It is the beginning of the ministry (service) He has placed within me. I know that I have been in ministry for years. But this one is different. He has been equipping and training me for this time. Lord, I need to hear every Word You utter, to feel You so close that I may do Your will. Lord, be glorified in this service to You. You trust me to be in the front to lead, I trust You to be in the front to lead me. Keep me humble, keep me anointed, keep me obedient, keep me connected to Your Power, and keep me protected. Hide me under Your wings while I do Your will. Heal them as they come. Teach them as they listen and deliver them as they open their hearts to You.

There is no turning back after this service. Move forward, take the cross I have to bear and move forward. Let them see You, Lord, and not me. Let Your Name be glorified throughout the land. I am a vessel and You are the One who made the vessel. You are the One who used the vessel. Like a vase, the owner put water in it to water the plant. He put His word in me to water His people. He used a pot to plant flowers. He uses me to plant His word. But God gives the increase. He makes the flowers and plants grow. He makes His people grow in Spirit and truth.

## Scriptures:

Give to the Lord the glory due His name; bring an offering and come before Him; oh, worship the Lord in the beauty of holiness. 1 Chronicles 16:29 (NKJV)

Shout joyfully to the Lord, all the earth breaks forth in song, rejoice and sing praises. Psalm 98:4 (NKJV)

I thank You, Lord, for restoration and resurrection.

# Trust Journey

**December 14, 2010**

Although I feel that God has made a change in my life, the evidence is still not in line with those changes. I need to have faith and believe those things He promised. I know that I know and there is no doubt that God has released the blessings, the anointing, the power for the next level and next dimension. No matter what it looks like, God has made it happen.

I keep telling myself, I must hold on. I must trust Him and believe Him. Watch it manifest before your eyes. God, my Father, has taken care of it all. The bills, sickness, ministry, provisions, peace, substance, and direction, He has opened the doors. He has made ways out of no way. He has closed doors I should not go through. If you want to stay in the will of God continue to have faith. May sure you continue to praise and worship Him. One important thing is to let God order your steps. Only God can help me through this journey. No one else can, even if they wanted to help me.

Trust in the Lord and lean not on your own understanding. You have to know that He is God. Without Him, I am nothing.

## Scriptures:

He will yet fill your mouth with laughing, and your lips with rejoicing. Job 8:21 (NKJV)

O Lord, our Lord, how excellent is Your Name in all the earth! Psalm 8:9 (NKJV)

Thank You, Lord.

# A Journey through Night Vision

**December 18, 2010**

I thought I was asleep but I was awake. I was headed one place but I ended up in another place. I kept trying to get to that place but I was going around in circles. I kept seeing the same people, the same school buses, and the same police officers working an accident.

I decided to get off that road. I did not know where I was going but I saw two people going the same way. They were nice and it felt good. We had to go through check points. These check points were in odd places. One was at someone's house and the other point was at a restaurant. We had to show a receipt or some type of paper giving us permission to go through the check points.

When I got to the check point at the restaurant, I did not have the receipt. But when I got to the checker he said, "I see you have it. Go ahead". So I went in. It was strange, I did not show him anything but he saw the receipt. He saw "it".

There was a couple managing the restaurant. Another young man was there also. A girl and the two people who were traveling with me went to the back of the restaurant. I was left alone with the guys. I felt uneasy at first until we started to talk. I ask the guy who managed the restaurant about his relationship with the girl. As I was asking the question, she came out and said that they were supposed to get married but she did not think he wanted to marry her. He admitted that he wanted to marry her and showed her paper he was writing on about her. He was explaining how he loves her.

Then I realized that I had left one of my bags somewhere. I kept running trying to go everywhere I had been to find the bag. Then I decided to check the last check point. They were holding it. I got it and went back to the restaurant. When I got there it was as if they were waiting on me. Two guys were on their knees. I went to them and put my hands on their head. They went down to the floor crying, confessing, and praying to God.

A woman from my past was there sitting on a chair talking. She was talking about me and when we finished, she said, "I should have gotten in that for a healing." I told her that she did not want a healing. She did not want me to touch her. She was there to bring me problems. Then, she disappeared. A young guy was there looking confused about everything going on. I asked him how old he was and about his relationship with the other guy. He was not related but he found a brother and father in those guys. God had revealed that He sent him a family to love him.

***REVELATION:***

When I got out of the bed, the lady in my past represented my past. A prophet has no honor in his home town. Well, she represented the past aches, pains, back biting, and rejections from church people. Also, the check points were different places I will go to or have been to doing the work of God. The past cannot stop the blessings of God. I have the power to shut up the enemy. I have to do God's work. I have the Spirit of God within me to deliver others. The harvest is plentiful and ready. The laborers are few but powerful if they are obedient.

We have to stop going down the wrong road. It will only take you in circles. You will see daily living without changes.

We have to let God guide us down the right road. We have what it takes to go through different levels. God goes into a place and out without any notice or advertisement. He goes in and performs miracles and goes out. God will send you a family if your biological family rejects you. Do not reject their love, it is God's love through a new family. I went through the check point without the require paper. I will have what I need to move forward. God will give me favor with man (human) to do His assignments.

I hear the Lord say, "Trust Me and do what I said to you". He has us in His hands. He has everything we need. No matter what happens, trust God.

## Scriptures:

Lead me, O Lord, in Your righteousness because of my enemies; make Your way straight before my face. Psalm 5:8 (NKJV)

The Lord is my light and my salvation; whom shall I fear? The Lord is the strength of my life; of whom shall I be afraid? Psalm 27:1 (NKJV

Thank You, Lord, for guidance. The steps of a good "man" are order by God. Order our steps, Lord.

# Lord, I thank You for My Journey

**December 27, 2010**

That is a song! I remember this song from my youth. I am not sure who wrote it.

Lord, I thank You
Lord, I thank You
For my journey
Lord, You brought me from a long, long way
Lord, I thank You
Lord, I thank You
For my journey
Lord, You brought me from a long, long way.

Then it says, "Had to cry sometimes" and "Had to pray sometimes".

I thought about this journey to this place in my life. I had to cry, pray, laugh, run, walk the floor, yell out, and more. But He brought me!

Think about your journey. No matter how you got there, no matter what happened, He brought you this far. And guess what? He will keep doing it.

Then I remember hearing:
Some said I wasn't going to make it
But You brought me.
Lord, You brought me from a long, long, way.

He prepares a table before me in the presence of my enemies. (Psalm 23:5a, NKJV) Some might have said I would not make it. But who cares?

God said He has a plan for my life, a plan of peace and no evil. This comes from the New King James Version in Jeremiah 29.

Lord, I thank You
Lord, I thank You
Lord, I thank You for my journey
You brought me from a long, long, way.

I thought about my sinful life style back "when". I mean the times I practiced sin. I was just doing my thing. Thank You, Lord, for protecting me from HIV/AIDS, alcohol poisons, alcohol addictions, and many other things which could have been results from my "sinful" life. Now I do not practice sin. I come short sometimes but I try to live holy and righteous.

I seek God for directions and guidance. I try to the best of my spiritual ability to follow His directions and guidance. Some do not understand but He does because He is directing.

Lord, forgive me for my short coming. The Bible states that we all come short. We can go to You and ask for forgiveness and get back on the right path.

I do not practice sin anymore. I practice loving when it is hard to love. I practice giving when it is hard to give. Then loving and giving becomes easier.

Praise the Lord!

**Scriptures:**

Oh, taste and see that the Lord is good; blessed is the man who trusts in Him. Psalm 34:8 (NKJV)

He made everything beautiful in its time. Ecclesiastes 3:11a (NKJV)

Finally, my brethren be strong in the Lord and in the power of His might. Ephesians 6:10 (NKJV)

Let us hear the conclusion of the whole matter: Fear God and keep His commandments, for this is man's all. Fort God will bring every work into judgment, including every secret thing, whether good or evil. Ecclesiastes 12:13-14 (NKJV)

Lord, I thank You. You brought me from a long, long way.

# A Trusting Journey

December 29, 2010

I know there will be more than one entry on the subject of trusting in this book. I hope you understand how important it is to trust God and His plan. I am in a place now that I have to trust God each day for provision. I cannot save stuff for the next week or the next day. I have to trust Him to provide each day's provision such as gas, food, bill money, etc.

When I did not know how I was going to pay for gas, He worked it out. He did not bring funds from the sky. He released my money earlier than I expected. He moves through people and computers. God has proven Himself again. He is in charge. He will always supply my needs. I just cannot do anything but thank Him. The whole state system was obedient to God to release money earlier. They could not explain what happened to the system. I got what I needed on time. He is a present help and an on time God.

I love Him so much and I know He loves me. I know He wants me to have everything I need. Seek Him first. He will take care of the rest. He knows what I need. I realized that I am in the "just enough" stage of my life. Just enough for this day. Just enough for this situation. Just enough grace. His grace is sufficient. That means His grace is the right amount for that time and situation. He is a present help. I will be in "more than enough" stage very soon. I have to stay focused on Him.

### Scriptures:

Rejoice in the Lord always, again I will say, rejoice! Philippians 4:4 (NKJV)

The Lord is your keeper; The Lord is your shade at your right hand. The sun shall not strike you by day nor the moon by night. Psalm 121:5-6 (NKJV)

Thank You, Lord, for providing for me daily. Nobody but You can do it.

# JOURNEY OF PURPOSE

## January 14, 2011

As I was riding to work, I heard a song which said, "I want to talk to You, Lord, so speak to me, Lord". The singer also said, "I need to hear from You." She continues, "I do not know what to do until You talk with me."

I remember how I was feeling last night and this morning. I began to feel that I am not going the right direction again. Now I see why the writer wrote, "Do not be weary in well doing." You can get weary and tired on this journey. I focused back on the song on the radio. It was as if the Lord put those words there because I did not know what to pray about that morning. I could not get the words to come out.

Wow! He answered me that quickly. He answered me while the song was playing. The Spirit reminded me of the time God told me the purpose of the ministry He has for me. After I got ordained, I was in a hotel room in Florida for annual training. The Lord spoke to me so clearly; it was amazing.

Three years before that day, or maybe 3.5 years before that date, God spoke to me while I was on my knees in Florida on another annual training. He told me to go out and teach His Word. I jumped off of my knees, looked around the room in amazement. I could not believe I heard a voice in the room and no one was there but me. I tried to reason with God and let Him know that I am the Sunday Superintendent, I am already teaching. I did not focus on the words, "go out". Later He directed me to get ordained. I did what He commanded like I did before. I asked Him, "Why?" God knows the heart of man. He will send me places where I will need that paper to open doors. He said that I needed the paper for man not Him. God knows man's (human) heart.

After I was ordained, I went to Florida again on annual training. The Lord spoke to me so clear. Just like Saul/Paul, He told me the ministry He placed within me. The instructions came in a period of three to five days. I remember the voice said:

> "You are My minister. You are a servant of the Lord. Minister means "servant". I want a servant who will do whatever I need to be done. Do not worry about title. Just do what I need at the time I need it. You will teach, preach, touch some, and I will heal through you. Whatever I need at the time, I want you to do. If I need you to prophesy, I want you to speak what I am saying. I want you go to the lost." As I was thinking something else, He said, "The lost is not what you think. I am talking about the ones who have a home. The ones I have called and chosen to do My will. Some of them you have to introduce to Me, some of them backslide, and some of them do not understand who I am in their lives. I need you to help them home. You have to belong to a home to be lost. I want you to worship Me in spirit and truth." He went on to say, "Do not let anyone label you; you are My servant, a minister of God."

I just thought about that time while the song was playing. These words were given to me during that weekend. If you seek God, He will be found. God spoke so clearly to me that weekend, it was amazing. I know some do not believe but I know what I know. I received my purpose that day. It was in April 2005. He ordained me for a purpose. He saved me for a purpose. I was confused a little because people who I trust were guiding me to a certain ministry but God said that whatever He wants, I need to do. If that is the assignment for the time, He will guide me there. Then if He needs me for another task or assignment, He will direct me there, too.

Saul was on the road to Damascus when he had an encounter with Jesus. Later, God told Ananias to go to Saul. He told Ananias to go to Saul and that Saul is a chosen vessel, that Saul would bear His Name before Gentiles, kings, and the children of Israel. God also said He would show Saul how many things he must suffer for God's Name sake. In Acts 26:16-18, Paul told them about the encounter he had with Jesus. Saul was told to rise and stand on his feet for He had appeared to him for this purpose to make him a minster and a witness to the things God reveal to him. God would use Saul to open their eyes in order to turn them from darkness to light and from the power of satan to God that they may receive forgiveness of sins and an inheritance among those who are sanctified by faith in Him.

Paul knew what God had called him to do. He later told King Agrippa what he experienced. In other words, Paul did what God called him to do. We have purpose so we have to do what God has called us to do. Ask Him to show you and tell you. Stay in the word, stay in prayer with Him, and stay focused on His will. Glory to God! Glory to God1

**Scriptures:**

Now faith is the substance of things hoped for, the evidence of things not seen. Hebrews 11:1 (NKJV)

Let not your heart be troubled; you believe in God believe also in Me. John 14:1 (NKJV)

Let your light shine before men, that they may see your good works and glorify your Father in heaven. Matthew 5:16 (NKJV)

But seek first His kingdom and His righteousness, and all these things will be added to you. Matthew 6:33 (NKJV)

Thank You, Lord, for reminding me of the purpose. Jesus left the Holy Spirit here to teach and guide us. He will also bring things to our remembrance. He did it for me.

# A Revelation Journey

January 14, 2011

I see so many people sick and having surgeries. Heart and back surgeries mostly. One person I know was having a heart surgery. I asked God for a word of comfort to give to that person. I remember hearing, "God wants your heart healthy." He wants you to forgive others. He wants you to let go of the pains, rejections, and unforgiveness in your heart. Ask God to clean and heal your heart in the natural and in the spirit. I do not know if they prayed for these things or not. But they had the natural surgery through God and they are recovering well. Praise God!

Our hearts are filled with unforgiveness. We go to church weekly with hard hearts. We are singing in choirs and telling others to live right but in our hearts, we have unforgiveness. We have to let go and ask God to help us forgive others, like He forgive us. The Holy Spirit wants to live in us. He wants to fill us with Himself. We have to let Him have room in our temple.

Forgive us our sin, iniquities, and transgressions as we forgive others of their sins, iniquities, and transgressions against us. Love our enemies and do good to those who hate us. Pray for those who use us and persecute us. Like Matthew 5:44-45 (NKJV) says, "That you maybe sons of Your Father in heaven". No one said it would be easy but "do able" in the Name of Jesus Christ.

If your heart is hard and cold; ask God to turn it to flesh again. Your natural heart pumps blood through your whole body. What is in your soul will affect your whole life and the body of Christ.

## Scriptures:

Ask and it will be given to you; seek and you will find; knock and it will be opened to you. Matthew 7:7 (NKJV)

If we confess our sin, He is faithful and just to forgive us our sins and to cleanse us form all unrighteousness. I John 1:9 (NKJV)

Thank You, Lord for forgiving us and please give us a forgiving heart.

# Journey of Revelation

## "Exposing Truth"

### January 17, 2011

Today, we celebrate the birth and life of Dr. Martin L. King. A man who was beaten, jailed, and persecuted for wanting everyone to love each other as the Lord had commanded. It was not about color but about love. Love is what God commanded and expected of us. We are to love all humans not just certain ones. We are to love whether they are rich, poor, tall, short, lean, fat, black, white, Chinese, Indians, male, female, drunk or sober. It is amazing how we justify our wrongness, our sins, and our disobedience. I cannot love them because they are ________________. (You fill in the blank.) I did not read that you cannot love because they are __________________________. You might not love their actions or their behavior but you have to love them. Some of us love dogs, cats, and even snakes more than the children in the streets or the elders who stays in our neighborhood.

My mother asked one of my grand-nieces if she was going to march today. She replied, "Martin Luther King already marched." That statement had me thinking. He already did the work. He already suffered for the cause. We do not need to march anymore. We need to love; we need to do what he was trying to put in place in the past. We are marching and still not loving.

Matthew 5:44 (NKJV) says it all, "We have heard to love your neighbor and hate you enemy." This is Jesus talking, "But I say to you, love your enemies, bless those who curse you, do good to those who hate you, and pray for those who spitefully use you and persecute you." We sit in church preaching, teaching, singing, ushering, dancing, and sleeping but are not following that great commandment. There is no excuse or justification for not loving. So as we thank God for a new year, as we think about what Dr.

Martin L. King was trying to do, as we try to tell people about Jesus, let's think about our love walk.

God exposed truth when He let President Obama in to office. I saw that much hatred was still in the nation. I saw it on the government level and individual level. I was attacked with words because of the winning of Presidency. The person did not know who I voted for. He just knew I was the same race as President Obama so he made negative remarks. Some people were so angry that they could not control their behavior anymore. It was not because he was a criminal or because they found a very dark past. Not because he cheated on his wife like some other presidents did before him. They were upset because they were exposed. They were exposed of pretending to love. They were pretending to love everyone but they did not. Their hearts were exposed. A fifth – grader said to my grand-niece that she would hurt Obama if she could. I did not report it because I knew she was just acting out what she had been exposed to about the election. After meeting her parents, I could tell that they were upset and frustrated about the presidency too. They might not have admitted to do harm to the president, however, they talked about him badly so she felt he was a threat to her family and the nation. He was in office about 15 days. She heard so many negative things that she thought he was a monster who was making her daddy upset, mad, and sad every day. We have to watch what we say and how we react to things and people. Our children do not understand when we are just talking or voicing our opinions. They could take those negative frustrations and hurt others. We have to find ways to be upset that will not produce a child killer. The result could be very dangerous. The other children were yelling and telling her that she does not know what she was talking about. So parents, our children are the results of our soil we plant them in. If we plant them in hatred and violence, then that is what will be in their hearts and minds. (Think about it, bullies.)

Truth has been exposed in the nation. God said that if you say you love Him and hate your brother (human), then you are a lie. He made all of us in His image. He did not say, "I made the white man, the black man, the tall man, the smart man, or the thin man in Our image," but He said, "Let us make man in Our image." (Genesis 1:26-27 NKJV) He commanded us to love. He did not suggest it.

Think about it, then go and ask for forgiveness. Change your ways and love, love, love. There is no way around it.

**Scriptures:**

Oh, come; let us sing to the Lord! Let us shout joyfully to the Rock of our salvation. Psalm 95:1 (NKJV)

Bless the Lord, O my soul! O Lord my God, You are very great; You are clothed with honor and majesty. Psalm 104:1 (NKJV)

Thank You, Lord, for revealing our sins and dark places. Forgive us.

# On A Journey

**January 18, 2011**

I am waiting for a co-worker to meet me today. While I am waiting, I am thinking about where I read in the Bible of how David behaves wisely when God was equipping him to become king. God allows things to happen and David behaves wisely. This does not mean that he did not do things that God did not approve. He did but God let him know it was wrong and David asked to be forgiven and went in the right direction. We have to ask for wisdom from God. We have to behave wisely in good and bad times. We have to know that God is watching and wants to direct our path.

We have to do like Paul told Timothy to do. He told him to be mindful of his conduct and words. We have to be mindful of our reactions as well as our actions on this journey.

If we lack wisdom, we need to ask God for wisdom. Look at the first chapter in James. He will give it to us. If we have His wisdom, we can behave wisely.

SCRIPTURES:

The Lord is my shepherd; I shall not want. Psalm 23:1 (NKJV)

Trust in the Lord and do good; dwell in the land and feed on His faithfulness. Delight yourself also in the Lord, and He shall give you the desires of your heart. Psalm 37: 3-4 (NKJV)

Lord, I want to behave wisely. I want You to guide me, to lead me, to order my steps.

# A Journey Worth Mentioning

## January 29, 2011

The week has been long due to the early rising and long trips throughout the week. God has blessed me so much; it is hard to explain. I cannot show much material manifestation of His blessings because I do not own much, but the Spiritual blessings are much. I thank Him for moving when I was weary, moving when the enemy was whispering. I thank God for moving when I did not see the way out. God keeps His promises. He will never leave nor forsake us. He did not do it last week or last year. I thought about how I could have been homeless twice in 2010. I never knew when they would say you have to go or to get out. That was a bad feeling and a bad way to live each day. Waiting on someone to say that they do not want you to live with them anymore. It happened twice that I had to go. Whether I was prepared or not, I had to go. But God was ready. He is always ready for our next move. He is ready for our trials and tribulations. He is ready for our disappointments and mistakes. Our God is always ready. What a Mighty God!

In this place, I am not talking about the "physical". He is ready to move me forward. He prepared my next move. I have to be ready to react when He acts. Do not look at others. Do not listen to others, but react to His move in my life by praying, obeying, seeking, sacrificing, listening, and loving. Wow!

That was good. Thanks Holy Spirit for that.

### Scriptures:

And we know that all things God work together for good to those who love God, to those who are called according to His purpose. Romans 8:28 (NKJV)

The eternal God is your refuge, and underneath are the everlasting arms. He will thrust out the enemy from before you, and will say, "Destroy!" Deuteronomy 33:27 (NKJV)

Thank You, Lord, for making plans for us. Thank You for being Omnipresent.

# A Morning's Journey

**January 30, 2011**

I woke up this morning with my mind on Jesus. That is a song. I can say for the last 2 months I really have been waking up with my mind on Jesus. I have to get up and spend some time with Him. I get revived and strength when I spend some time with Him. It seems as if I only go to work, go to visit papa, and go home. I get up, pray, read, dress; then off to work I go. The ride is fulfilling most of the time because I get another chance to talk with the Father. Five days of week, this is the routine. I guess I miss the time when I have different assignments each day. Do not get me wrong, I love my job but sometimes I feel that I am in bondage because I have to be at a certain place five days a week at the same time. If I want to go take someone out to breakfast, to pray with them and encourage them, I could not because I am obligated to be at work at a certain time.

The creative side of me wants a chance to grow even more. I have restrictions on what to do and how to do it on man's job. Structure is good but some of us want to be more creative, more flexible, and more moveable.

When you cannot be yourself, you feel as if you are dying or starving inside. I had this feeling before at a church. God gave me ideas, programs, and other visions but I was bound so I could not do them. I will not leave the job. I thank God for it. I will not leave until His says so. I have enough sense to know that. But if He says go, believe me, I will go. If He keeps me there, I will take advantage of that blessing. You see, God knows how He created each one of us. He has a plan for our lives that will glorify Him. We need to operate in our gifts and talents that He placed in us when the opportunity comes.

## Scriptures:

Have I not commanded you? Be strong and courage; Do not be afraid, nor be dismayed, for the Lord your God is with you wherever you go. Joshua 1:9 (NKJV)

You will show me the path of life; In Your presence is fullness of joy; At Your right hand are pleasures forevermore. Psalm 16:11 (NKJV)

Thank You, Lord, for an opportunity to worship You.

# Journey of a Different Life

**February 2, 2011**

I went to Bible study at a local church. The pastor was talking about how we speak and what we speak can destroy lives. We can speak "death" or "life" in our lives. We need to speak "life" and have it in our hearts and minds that God will keep every promise that He has made. He will not go back on His word. Lord forgive me for any unbelief and doubt. I will walk in faith. I will watch what I say about myself and others. Faith the size of a mustard seed is what it takes to move a mountain. God's super with our natural is "supernatural." He does not have to work hard to make blessings flow. He just speaks it into existence. We need to do the same and speak "life" into existence.

Love, it's yours
Peace, it's yours
Mercy, it's yours
Grace, it's yours
Good health, it's yours
Obedience children, it's yours
A home, it's yours
A car, it's yours
More power, it's yours
More of Him, it's yours

Ask and it shall be given. Abide in Him and His word and He will abide in you. God said it and that is enough! It is time for us to believe and trust Him. We need to trust His plan for our lives. God is Almighty and All Knowing. He knows what we need. So why not trust Him. Just focus on Him and His Word. Start quoting scriptures and singing praises when bad and negative ideas come into your head. Watch what happens! Submit to God, resist the devil and he will flee.

**The scriptures below says it very well.**

**Scriptures:**

He will yet fill your mouth with laughing and your lips with rejoicing. Job 8:21 (NKJV)

Give to the Lord the glory due His name. Bring an offering and come before Him; oh, worship the Lord in the beauty of holiness. 1 Chronicles 16:29 (NKJV)

Let us therefore come boldly to the throne of grace that we may obtain mercy and find grace to help in time of need. Hebrews 4:16 (NKJV)

Thank You, Lord, for Your love, peace, and grace.

# A Day's Journey

**February 3, 2011**

It's another day's journey; I'm glad about it.

It was a day of uplifting and encouragement. He has filled me with His Spirit. He has protected me all day and all night. He has provided all that I need. After talking with one of my customers today, I thought about how we put too much focus on money and how much money we spend on our birthday. We want to go way out for our birthday. We want to spend money and do it up but we do not think about Who brought us to this day.

She was upset because she paid her bills and did not have money to spend for her birthday. You know what? There are some of us who want to have money to pay the bills. (Huh)

Birthdays are just another day that the Lord has blessed us, especially if we have a chance to get it right before we die. If we are healthy that is even better. If we are filled with the joy of the Lord, that is even better.

We need to get our minds renewed to the right place and to the right Person. Our minds need to be on the Person who allowed us to be born. (Huh)

Birthdays are days God performed a miracle! So thank Him for bringing us in this world to do His will.

### Scriptures:

For as the body without the spirit is dead, so faith without works is dead also. James 2:26 (NKJV)

So you may walk in the way of goodness, and keep to the paths of righteousness. Proverbs 2:20 (NKJV)

Thank You, Lord. You gave me food to eat; I am glad about it.

# Morning's Journey

**February 5, 2011**

A journey of the mind!

This morning, I am not moving or going anywhere physically. I am moving in my mind. Looking at "opportunities" and thinking about directions and situations. You know what I mean when I say I start thinking about "if I should have done this" or "if I should have not done that?" I know that the enemy is trying to stop a plan. He is trying to stop God's plan for my life and others' lives too. But God!

God will ensure His plan will be fulfilled. He knows all the tricks and schemes the enemy tries to do. I thank God for watching and protecting me. Wow! I also thank Him for providing for me. Things are not as I want them to be this hour, however, they will be before the day ends, because God is always right on time. He provides our needs and I need His provision today. Thank You, Lord.

My mind journeyed back to the Navy Reserves because I was working on my resume for a job. Sometimes we think we are doing something for one reason and God is allowing us to do it for another reason. The old saying goes, "Father knows best," well Father (the Lord) knows best. We have to trust Him.

Thank You, Lord for closing doors.
Thank You, Lord for opening doors.
Thank You, Lord for being in control.
Thank You, Lord for the things that never been told.

**SCRIPTURES:**

Set your mind on things above, not on things on the earth. Colossians 3:2 (NKJV)

Likewise the Spirit also helps in our weaknesses. Romans 8:26a (NKJV)

God, let Your word be a light which lead me on the path of righteousness.

# See with My Spiritual Eyes

**February 7, 2011**

Fill me, Lord
I need an fresh anointing upon me

Show me, Lord
I want to see a miracle from You

Wash me, Lord
I want to be pure and holy

Touch me, Lord
I need to feel Your loving kindness

Do it, Lord
Give me what You promised me

Do it, Lord
That I may see

**Scripture:**

One thing I desired of the Lord that will I seek; that I may dwell in the house of the Lord all the days of my life, to behold the beauty of the Lord, and to inquire in His temple. Psalm 27:4 (NKJV)

Thank You, Lord, for doing it for me and others.

# A Journey of Hopelessness

**February 27, 2011**

I talked with saints this week who feel that they have no hope. They are upset because they do not have money to pay bills. I heard things from "why me", "did I do something wrong", "I been praying", "I am tired of waiting", "I am going to lose all my things", "I have a house in foreclosure" and more.

Those statements ran in my mind for a few hours. I had to go before my Father and ask Him for help for them. We are being strengthened in our faith. We have to hold on to our faith that God will come on time. We have to believe enough that we are willing to serve Him, even when all our earthly possessions are gone.

God knows our struggles. He knows our pains. He knew Job's struggles and pains. He loves us. It is hard to believe when someone else is telling you to hang-on. It will be alright. We have to serve Him whether or not we have a house. When we are healed or sick, we still need to serve Him. We have to believe what we have been telling people before it happens to us. God will provide: He will never leave you or forsake you. He is working it out.

Father, I bring them to You. I believe for them that You are working it all out. I believe You know what they are going through and You already have a plan for them. Once again, Lord, glorify Yourself. Make Yourself known in their lives.

## Scripture:

Hear, O Lord, when I cry with my voice! Have mercy also upon me and answer me. When You said, "Seek My face," my heart said to You, "Your face, Lord, I will seek." Psalm 27:7-8 (NKJV)

Thank You for provisions. Thank You for peace and joy. I thank You for love.

# Seeking Your Face

**February 27, 2011**

Seeking Your face
Seeking Your presence
Seeking Your mercy
Seeking Your grace

Walking in faith
Walking in love
Walking in holiness
Walking in grace

Believing Your promises
Believing Your word
Believing Your covenant
Believing Your Spirit

Scripture:

But the hour is coming and now is when the true worshipers will worship the Father in spirit and truth; for the Father is seeking such to worship Him. John 4:23 (NKJV)

Seek Him while He can be found. We need Him every day.

# Journey from Idolatry to God

## March 26, 2011

I know that God allows things to happen in our life for various reasons. When I had my son, I felt I had everything I needed in life. Later I joined the Navy; my son was taken from me while I was in boot camp. I went to court two times before I got custody again. I went to court against the step-mother while the father was not able to take care of him. I had so much hatred in my heart. I went to work for12 hours without remembering how I got there or what happened during the day. I would cry and go to the bathroom and wipe my eyes then go back to work. I received awards for outstanding work and did not remember anything I did. All I wanted was my son back. I could not eat or live. I did not let anyone close to me. I just wanted my son. I remember saying before I got in the military that I did not care if the world dies as long as my son and I were together. I also said things like if my son and I could live on an island alone, I would visit my mother once a month. I was so wrapped up in him that I "worshipped" him. I did not know that I had made him my idol, my god.

I believed in Jesus, but I put Him after my child. Then one day, I did not have him anymore. I thank God that He did not let him die but He let him be apart from me so I could realize Who my true God is. I lost custody for small stupid reasons. One reason was because I was in the military. Now I know the that true reason was that I needed to get focused on Who my God is. He is a jealous God and He will not have any god before Him.

I remember asking God for my son and He told me to get that hatred out of my heart. Some of you think you have hate but hatred will consume you. It will make you think of nothing but killing that person. I had real hatred. But God! I went to a church in Chesapeake, Virginia. I began to develop love for God in my heart from Bible study and the love the people of the church gave me. I did not know this was the beginning journey back to Jesus. I never asked the pastor or members to pray that I get my son back but I went to church and received the Word.

Later I went overseas and one day I picked up the Bible off my night stand. I always kept it there but did not read it too much. Late one night I began to read it and it began to change something within me. I was reading Psalm 51 every night. Each night I read it, I got a different revelation. I began to reject some of the things I was doing. I did not understand it but just noticed a change in me. I started to think differently and reacting differently.

When I returned to the states I went back to the same church in Virginia. The pastor and members remembered me. I was gone three years. I was welcomed by the church members along with my son. God was my lawyer when I went to court the last time. I made Him my Lord and Redeemer. He represented me when I needed it. Praise God! That was easy money for the lawyer I hired. God already set it up for us. The last time I was in court for about five minutes. The judge called me to the front along with the caregiver. He asked one question, "Do you have a place to live?"

When I got custody of him, I inherited his issues. Someone treated him badly in the last place he stayed. We made it through one barrier at a time. God gave us a second chance to be together. We enjoyed each other and praised God together. We had a great church family in Virginia who supported us and loved us.

When I made God my God and surrendered to Him, the void that was in me was filled. I feel as if nothing is missing in my life. My son has a void in him also. He must realize God is the only One Who can fill that void. I pray that he realizes it before he gets old so he could be energized and young to be used by God. There is no one or nothing that could fill that void. Everywhere I went and everything I did was not enough. But now I do not have many material things but the void is filled and I know that is because I have a relationship with the Father.

God allowed my world to be stirred up because He wants to be first. I am grateful for His plan in my life. I do not understand everything He is doing but I trust Him to take care of me.

A great poem came out of the separation from my son. "Thank You for my Son" was an emotional poem I wrote. The miles and the heart aches did not stop me from still loving my child.

God gets the glory for my life. God gets the glory for our lives.

**SCRIPTURES:**

Create in me a clean heart, O God, and renew a steadfast spirit within me. Do not cast me away from Your presence, and do not take Your Holy Spirit from me. Psalm 51:10-11 (NKJV)

O Lord, open my lips, and my mouth shall show forth Your praise. Psalm 51:15 (NKJV)

Thank You, Lord, for Your Son. Thank You, Lord, for my son. Thank You for a church family who loved me when I needed it most. All the glory goes to You.

# Journey to Pine Mountain

**April 29, 2011**

My brother and I rode to Pine Mountain for our mother's birthday celebration. I was uncomfortable about the trip at first. It was getting dark and I have not been there in a long time. Also, I was getting tired. I wanted to be home in bed. It was not a long trip. We talked and made it safely. I had something pressing on my mind but I knew it was not the time to say it. Waiting on God, I just prayed that God would reveal the truth while he was traveling on the road tomorrow alone.

Most of the people are coming tomorrow. However, I do not believe they all will come. It seems to be a good crowd tonight. My uncle is here and that is a blessing.

I pray that God manifest Himself on this trip. Thank You, Lord, for the protection and mercy all day and night. I hope to finish writing this book on this trip. We got here late so my brother did not have time to socialize with mom. He was too tired so he went to bed.

Looking at this house, I see simplicity. It is not decorated beautiful like many of the ones we rented before. I have not felt at ease about the place yet. I have to sit and pray and see what happens. Lord, fill this place with Your Spirit. Make it Your sanctuary. It would be nice to be here alone to write, think, and have peace. Better enjoy it tonight because the place will be full tomorrow, hopefully with laughter, I can get peace and quiet at home.

The family gatherings have changed. We used to sing hymns for a long time. A couple of us started one but others will not sing along with us. Their focus was not on praising God on this trip.

**Scripture:**

Praise the Lord! Praise the name of the Lord! Praise Him, O you servants of the Lord! Psalm 135 (NKJV)

Thank You, Lord, for another healthy year with my mom.

# Journey to the Underlining Truth

**May 10, 2011**

I noticed here at this conference that you hear God's Name in the introductions and in the remarks. However, I do not see things operating according to God's Word. I pray they are going to be operating according to God's plan.

I heard how "blessed" we are many times. I wonder if we know or should I say if we really know how blessed we really are? Some of us were in war. Some of us served only during peace time. But we are still "blessed." As we were talking, we identified problems, issues, and barriers that our customers deal with on a daily basis. We have created theories and concepts to assist people through those issues. However, in the "real" world, they are not working. Some abuse the system, some are not getting enough assistance, and some are denied assistance even though they need it.

The numbers are saying those theories and concepts are working. However, being in the "real" world, they are not working effectively. They are not working enough to see a large number (100%) get what they need. I know we say there will never be 100% of any problem that will be solved. Too many factors are involved. But we have to stop saying I am sorry. Yes, you are homeless but unless you have some income coming in, we cannot work with you. Well hello, they probably do not need us if they have income. What to do about their children? Give them to foster parents and leave the mother homeless is not the answer. Put them in a foster home to be abused? Not all of them but some. How do we help those who were rejected or lacking sufficient services? Where is the program for them? Prayer has to be in place. We have to really know what it means to be "blessed", to use God's Name.

The word below gave us the answer. Let us "fear" the Lord. Let us give Him reverence and honor that is due to Him.

**Scripture:**

Behold, how good and how pleasant it is for brethren to dwell together in unity! Psalm 133:1 (NKJV)

Thank You, Lord, for shelter. Help us to help others.

# A Journey with God in Peace

**May 27, 2011**

Lord kept me in peace. I would not say I was in perfect "peace". Wow! Fiery darts were thrown at me today! I had one hit after another. I will admit that I vented some but for the most part I withstood the scheme of the enemy. He used a couple of people but I have to say that the Holy Spirit held my tongue. Thanks again God.

I have to believe and trust that this too shall pass.

God loves me. He knows what is going on. I have to stay focused and love those who treat me wrong and pray for them. Forgive them Lord they know not what they are doing. Help them to love and encourage others. Most of all, Father let Your will be done.

It will all work out for my good because I love Him and am called for His purpose. And because He promise me a future and a hope, not of evil but peace!

He is the Prince of Peace. I am in the family of the Prince of Peace. Amen, Amen!

Thank You, Lord for reminding me of whose family I am in.

I walk in victory daily if I keep my mind on Him Who keeps me in perfect peace.

I put on the whole armor of God daily. I am glad He put that in my morning devotion. I need to be able to stand when the enemy throws his fiery darts.

## Scriptures:

You will keep him in perfect peace, whose mind is stayed on You, because he trusts in You. Isaiah 26:3 (NKJV)

And seek the peace of the city where I have caused you to be carried away captive, and pray to the Lord for it; for in its peace you will have peace. Jeremiah 29:7 (NKJV)

The Lord is my Shepherd; I shall not want. Psalm 23:1 (NKJV)

Thank You, Lord, for being my shield. Thank for the Word.

# He was There

He was there when you first said hello
He was there when you first laughed together
He was there when you asked for advice
He was there when you left home
He was there when you felt alone
He was there when pain was present
He was there when trouble arise
He was there when you could not
He was there when she took her first breath
He was there when she took her last breath
He was there when you said good-bye
He was there and now she is with Him

Scriptures:

"Look!" he answered, "I see four men loose, walking in the midst of the fire; and they are not hurt, and the form of the fourth is like the Son of God." Daniel 3: 25 (NKJV)

Yea, though I walk through the valley of the shadow of death. I will fear no evil; for You are with me; Your rod and Your staff, they comfort me. Psalm 23:4 (NKJV)

Thank You, Lord, for never leaving me. I am thankful to be able to feel Your presence throughout my days.

# I Came to Thee while on this Journey

**September 29, 2011**

Well I am in Columbus. I am living in a small apartment. I am alone in this city with a new job and a new apartment. But I will say, I am still feeling the Holy Spirit. I am feeling His power more these last few days than ever. God, I am Your child and I am seeking Your face, directions, and plans for my journey. I know You are working it all out while I am waiting for you. Lord, I thank You for my bed, furniture, and resources. I know You will take care of me.

I have a crazy praise and cannot stop. Holy is my God. I need Thee, Lord, I need Thee. Every hour I need Thee. Oh, bless me now my Savior. I come to Thee. I do not know Your plan but I know I trust Your plan.

I trust You to protect me.
I trust You to direct me.
I trust You to teach me.
I trust You to guide me.
I trust You to keep me.

**Scripture:**

For we know that all things work together for good to those who love God, to those who are the called according to His purpose. Romans 8:28 (NKJV)

Thank You, Lord, for being a Faithful God. I feed on Your faithfulness.

# JOURNEY TO ANOTHER CITY

**October 23, 2011**

I have been here for at least a month now. I need to adjust to a new city to live in and a new job. I will say it has been interesting to be here. I have been isolated mostly but it is a good thing. I just got to know that it is all about Him. I am watching and taking notice of my surroundings. These are moments, where listening is more important than talking or doing. As I sat here looking at the hill in front of my apartment; I see the glory of God in the trees, bushes, and the hill. The area is quiet. The sun is shining and the hill is bright from the sun. It stands out more than anything around me.

I heard about "transition" when I first got here. Now I hear about "blessing the works of your hands." I have to know that God will bless the works of your hands if you have given your life to Him to be used as His servant and child. Faith without works is dead. So now it is time to do the work. I am trying to move and move within His plan. I do not want to sit on His works but I do not want to move too fast. Each day is a little struggle to stay within His plan so I move very carefully and prayerfully.

Today was the first day I went to church here since I have been living here and it was very interesting. They were not having service but a birthday celebration. There was a celebration in the sanctuary today, not for Jesus but for one of the ministers. I saw many things in there and I saw some of the people there who were trying to praise God. They tried on several occasions to focus on God and His Word but someone would get up and talk about the birthday man. The worship service was canceled to have a birthday party for a minister. Huh? I could not stay for the whole celebration. I made my contact and went home. I was just sitting here wondering what to do now.

God will bless the works of my hands if I am working to glorify Him.

**Scripture:**

May He grant you according to your heart's desire, and fulfill all your purpose. Psalm 20:4 (NKJV)

Thank You, Lord, for giving me a chance to do the service You put in me. Please order my foot steps and guide me to that perfect will.

# A Journey of Dedication

**November 23, 2011**

I got a revelation on last Sunday about being dedicated to the Lord. We have to be dedicated to His Plan and to Him as our Savior and Creator. Even though we are going through trials and tribulations, we still have to dedicate our lives and gifts to His purpose. We can complain about not having enough of many things and not getting the healing we expect from God. We can complain about not having what we think we need. However, we cannot complain about Him keeping His promises. He did not say when it will happen but He promised to do it and He does not lie. Our relationship with the Father will open our eyes to know and see the promises He gave to us. To explain it better, if you have an intimate relationship (which is like a personal close relationship) with the Father, then you can know the promises God made to you. God is Sovereign and He blesses who He wants to bless. Some of our blessings come from obedience to Him. You have to seek the answers yourself about which one requires us to do something. I called them the "if you, then I" promises. I saw many of them in Job. Lately, I noticed a couple of them in I Kings about David and his descendants. For example, in I Kings 6:11-13, God told Solomon if he does a certain thing then He will perform His Word with him. Take the time out to read this yourself. There are other "if you, then I" promises in the Bible. We want God to do it all and we just sit back and reap all His glory and benefits. Remember faith without works is dead. How great is His mercy? He is keeping those promises which do not require anything from us. Even the sinful man is living and breathing. Some are living "large" on earth but they are not living for Him. His mercy is giving them a chance to know Him before their last breath or before He returns, whichever one comes first.

Dedicate your time and gifts to His plan while you are going through. Focus on His plan for His Kingdom while you are going through. I am talking about this because I am here now. I am waiting until my change comes but while I am waiting, I am dedicating my gifts and time to serve Him. I will reap the reward of those things when the transition is complete. I will admit I cried, complained, and felt isolated and alone for a while. But God, I have to say that again, but God. He spoke to me through His servant on several occasions about being in transition and giving God praise and service while you are going through the gate to your next assignment. This assignment is not like the past ones, it is the ONE THAT WILL SHIFT EVERYTHING IN MY LIFE. Wow, I will not think as before, I will not pray like before, I will not sing like before, I will not serve like before, I will not live like before, and I will not expect like before. I will know that I know that God has called me for such a time as this. I have to continue to dedicate myself to His plan. I am watching Him work things out before my eyes and I am amazed each time. He loves me and I have to believe it to get through the gate to my purpose.

We have to dedicate (give) our gifts, praises, and love to the Lord even in tough times. I will not say bad times because if God allows it, well, it might not be bad times but tough times. We have to believe in God and get through them. God is worthy to be praised in good, bad, tough, wonderful, cheerful, lonely, and confused times. We have to dedicate, sacrifice, and praise Him and we have to dedicate our gifts to Him and move forward. When we are dedicating, learning, training and equipping for that SHIFT, we will see the glory of God and His power. The place we live or operate will give us opportunities to utilize our gifts.

We dedicate our church and services often but we do not follow His plan for that church or services. God wants to be first in all we do here on earth. Action is better than talking. Show Him how important He is in your life by putting Him first.

**Scriptures:**

Commit your works to the Lord, and your thoughts will be established. Proverbs 16:3 (NKJV)

Commit your way to the Lord, Trust also in Him, and He shall bring it to pass. Psalm 37:5 (NKJV)

Lead me, O Lord, in Your righteousness because of my enemies; make Your way straight before my face. Psalm 5:8 (NKJV)

Thank You, Lord, for guiding me through my assignments. You are an Awesome God.

# A Prayerful Journey

## April 1, 2012

I am just sitting here listening to a wonderful song. As I was listening, I heard the voice of God say, "Pray and believe." He also said, "I will take care of all of your situations." The answers are in your prayers. Communicate with Him. Pray, pray, pray!

Pray and give it to God. Leave it there with Him.

We cannot quench the Holy Spirit. Have Your way, Lord. Let Your program come forward in this place, Lord. I notice that I am always praying for directions from God. I guess my natural make up is low self-esteem. I am always questioning what I am doing and if I am doing it right. But when I get directions from God and I know it is from Him, I move with confidence. Others see me and think I am always sure of myself when I preach or teach. They do not know that God came in and did a transformation that day. When you are about to be used by God, you develop some courage and boldness. After the event is over, I am back to the little "scary" girl that is not sure of who she is and what she is. Sounds crazy but I guarantee you that someone can understand what I am talking about. It does not mean I do not have a relationship with Him. It does not mean I do not trust Him. I just have to seek Him often, probably more than many of you.

Well, I was praying and the song gave me a confirmation to my prayer. The song, "Pray and Leave it to God" spoke to my spirit. The singer made that song as she was on a prayerful journey. I had to pray that the Lord will give her what she needs. Shower her with Your blessings.

**Scripture:**

Therefore do not cast away your confidence, which has great reward. For you have need of endurance, so that after you have done the will of God, you may receive the promise. Hebrews 10:35-36 (NKJV)

Thank You, Lord, for giving me courage and walking with me.

# A Rainy Journey

**April 4, 2012**

I remember thinking, "it is raining and I do not want to go anywhere. Now I have set up a birthday celebration for my daddy today. How could I miss it?"

I have created a comfort zone in this apartment and do not want to go anywhere unless I know the Lord is summoning me out. I put this celebration together and I have to attend. This is an example of compromising and giving up your time for the ones you love. Many relationships are not working effectively because we are selfish. I am noticing in some marriages that some spouses are not willing to make their lives uncomfortable for their relationships.

I had to get gas; my tank was on "E". Just to let you know how uncomfortable it was for me. So, I got wet pumping gas. I had to walk in the rain to get the discount on the gas. I wanted the blessing so I had to walk for it. (Funny to me.) We have to work sometimes to see our blessings. God has it set up and we have to work through our faith to receive them. I will promise you that the discount on the gas was worth the walk. The blessings from the work you put with your faith is worth the reward reveal. Praise God! I just have to laugh at that. Works without faith is dead. We do not work to get into heaven but we put our natural into work with our faith and watch God's blessings and promises come to past.

The rain might be falling in your life but you have to continue to walk. You have to continue to move forward in love and faith. Do not complain but praise as you are walking in the rain. Go when you are sick, go when you are without money or resources, and go when others want to stay. Go when death is around you, go when there is no support, and go when your children are acting like "themselves". The reward is greater!

I will admit that we had a great time at the celebration. The family time was a blessing for my daddy and he enjoyed himself. The staff told us they were blessed from our singing about our Lord. The rain stopped before I headed back home. We have to submit to God (show love to my daddy) and resist the devil (the rain and issues) and he will flee (leave).

## Scripture:

Therefore by Him let us continually offer the sacrifice of praise to God that is the fruit of our lips, giving thanks to His Name. Hebrews 13:15 (NKJV)

Thank You, Lord, for a raining journey, a reward journey and a blessed journey.

# A TWISTED JOURNEY

**September 28, 2012**

The journey to this new place was not easy but was guided by my Lord. I have been pressing through the uncertainties and the battles. Things were not 100 percent smooth but it was pleasant. But recently, a tornado came in a form of a person. It came and turned things around and upside down. It came and destroyed self-esteem, confidence, and dedication of the staff. I lost sight of who I was for a moment. I notice the damage on the others as they came in the door. Since I am on the other side of the storm, I can say BUT GOD. But God exposed the truth. That is why I always pray for truth to be revealed. The tornado is still moving but with our faith in God and the leading of the Spirit, we can keep it down without doing any major damage now. Truth has been revealed. Where lies were told, truth has been revealed. Where deceit has been planted, truth has been revealed. God is a God of truth, love and grace. He sent His Holy Spirit here and He is the Spirit of Truth.

We were in our peaceful little world and it came to destroy the peace and healing we were doing. We have to expect the enemy to come; he comes to kill, steal, and destroy. But we have to be ready all the time. This is a lesson for us to always put on the Armor of God. Ask God for discernment. When the enemy comes in like a flood, God will hold up a standard (banner) against him. I would love to teach on that now but we must move on. Beloved, give it all to God.

Give me strength, Lord, to handle this tornado like You instruct me to do it. Please do not let my flesh interfere with Your work. I know You have a plan and Your plan will come to full term. Your purpose will be completed. God can be glorified in our storms. We do not like the feeling but our spirit man can still rejoice in His power.

## Scriptures:

Yet in all these things we are more than conquerors through Him who loved us. Romans 8:37 (NKJV)

You have heard that it was said; you shall love your neighbor and hate your enemy. But I say to you, love your enemies, bless those who curse you, do good to those who hate you, and pray for those who spitefully use you and persecute you, that you may be sons of your Father in heaven, ...Matthew 5:43-48 (NKJV) {continue to read all the verses they are a blessing}

Thank You, Lord, for all Your blessings. Thank You for loving me and keeping me. Please order my footsteps.

# Unsettling Journey

**October 9, 2012**

I notice that I am getting a little restless here. I feel as if something is about to happen. The days are long and boring now. I feel as if something is missing from my days and my life now. I wake up on Monday hoping it was Friday. I know that this is not the way to live. I was created for a purpose and I need to find it now! I am too old to waste my days and years working and not doing what I am created to do.

I have to thank those who are making it uneasy to stay. I have to thank them for opening my eyes and reminding me of my mission. I know that I was put here for a temporary task. I completed my task and now it is time to move on.

The files are ready and the books are completed. Things are in order for my replacement. I have to leave them in order for the next person. I want them to have an easy start. My pictures are packed and most of them are home now. My mind is made up and my heart is at ease for the transition.

I am ready to take the next step. I am ready to do what You called me to do, Lord. Lead me and guide my footsteps so I can be in Your will. Please open the doors I should walk in and close the ones I am not supposed to walk through. I will teach Your word and do Your will.

This is a step that takes faith. It takes faith for me to walk from this "tangible" job to an "intangible" service for You. I am trusting in You to guide me throughout this service. I am depending on You to lead me and show me the way to go and how to do the things You require of me.

**Scripture:**

Lead me, O Lord, in Your righteousness because of my enemies; make Your way straight before my face. Psalm 5:8 (NKJV)

Thank You, Lord, for choosing me to do Your will.

# Journey to Another Level

**January 9, 2013**

I thought the news of quitting my job would shock my family but they were supportive. I know God is working in this event. I know it seems extreme to some and crazy to others but I have to do what God called me to do. God called us for different administrations and to do different things on earth. Some people are to teach and preach God's word on a full-time basis without a "traditional" job. We have to know what God wants us to do and do it. I asked God a long time ago to use me for His glory. I am a living sacrifice for the glory of God. I do not have a job but I will admit I have peace.

If we are sold out to do God's will and follow His directions, He will work things out for us. I feel it is already completed for me. I am a teacher of the Most High God. I am not boasting but I am speaking what He told me. I wrestled in the beginning and I was afraid of the calling on my life. But now I am teaching His word more and more. I am in various cities teaching His word and I will admit, I feel free and peaceful. I do not feel as if I am in bondage like I did on my jobs. It was not the people or the money but the chains on me to be at a certain place at a certain time. I was not able to be free to do what was in my heart. Some people might think I am boasting but I am stating facts. It took me a long time to stand up and say that I am a teacher of the Most High God. I will say this also, that I am a child of the True Living God, Who created the heavens and earth. If you do not know who you are then the enemy can play with your head. I know because he did it to me for many years because I did not know who I am. I am the head and not the tail. I am someone special. You are special and you are made the way God wanted to make you. Do not apologize for being you. I just learned that this year. Now I am walking in my purpose.

My purpose is in levels and now I am in the right level at the right time with the right gifts and the right anointing. Wow! He just gave me that!

I praise God for the gift He has given me. I ask God to continue to order my steps and put me in the purpose He created me for on this earth. I have to stand faithful and believe every step of the way. We have to know that God is part of our lives every day and every moment. He shows me often His hands in my routine days. Look for His presence in your day. Do not seek Him just when you go to church or when a tragic thing happens.

There are times when I only have a little food. I never thought I would be so grateful for ten dollars' worth of food. It might sound sad but it was a great revelation for me. God will provide what I need at the time I need it. He is a present help. God is showing me that He is my Provision. He uses people to bless me and I do not have to ask them. I just go to Him and pray. There were times when I did not ask but just looked in the cabinets and He took take care of my need. I will say like David said, "I am glad I was afflicted." In my needs and afflicting, I got to know more of about God and His love. I learned how to live with much and now I know how to live with a small amount. Whatever state I am in, I praise God. He wants our attention on Him even through the storms.

I remember one day I was craving for something and He sent it by someone. My God will supply all my needs and give me some of my desires. I am amazed often at His works. Not from doubt but from pure excitement. Glory to God Almighty!

Through this event of my life, I walk by sight. I would be depressed and worry about what will happen to me. But now I do not worry because I walk by faith. It did not happen overnight to be able to walk by faith. It took trusting God with others situations and events throughout my life. I remember giving away half of my check to someone when I was not working. I had to pray and ask God is that really Him telling me to do it. I asked because I did not want to do it. You know we will ask God again if we do not want to do something. I did not give it to the person the first time God told me to do it. But afterward, I felt very bad and disconnected. I promised God that if He would give me another chance I would give it to her and I did. I was blessed beyond what I gave her. We have to trust God with our little and our abundance. **Everything belongs to Him anyway!**

My next level might not be the same as your next level but we all will have to go higher in this walk of faith. Each level will come with challenges of its own. We have to have more faith for each level. God will be there for each level and each round. Hold on to His hands.

**Scriptures:**

He will yet fill your mouth with laughing and your lips with rejoicing. Job 8:21 (NKJV)

But the Lord stood with me and strengthened me, so that the message might be preached fully through me and that all the Gentiles might hear. Also I was delivered out of the mouth of the lion. And the Lord will deliver me from every evil work and preserve me for His heavenly kingdom. To Him is glory forever and ever. Amen! II Timothy 4:17-18 (NKJV)

Thank You, Lord, for love, power, and a sound mind.
Thank You, Lord, for protecting and keeping me.
Thank You, Lord, for my food.
Thank You, Lord, for providing for me.

# Reflection Journey

## January 13, 2013

I was thinking about how depressed I used to be in the past. I would lie in the bed all day. I would sometimes get up and take a shower and put more sleeping clothes on, then get back into the bed. I did this for years and no one really knew how depressed I was. I thought about killing myself so many times. I did not want the shame if I failed. But most of the times, I thought about how my mom would be hurt. I acted as if I had it all together but I was so "empty" inside. I felt as if I did not belong anywhere. I felt like a stranger in my home when I was a child. My family loved me and I am sure of that but I always felt that it was more to me than beneath the eyes. I felt "empty" everywhere I went including the military. I carried that "empty" shell around for years.

The only joy that came to me was when I had my son. I believe I made him my god because I did not feel I needed anyone or anybody when I had him. Later God allowed him to be taken away from me. I can say now that I worshipped my son. I always said he and I could live on an island alone and visit my mom once or twice a year. People got on my nerves I "thought". Now I know I was just having a problem within me and it filtered out to others. It was me that got on my nerves. I made bad choices and suffered from them. Then I got upset at everyone else.

I accepted Christ as my Savior at a young age and was filled with the Holy Spirit. I had two spirits fighting inside of me. The Holy Spirit really was not fighting He was chastening me about my decisions while my fleshy spirit (Adamic) was trying to lead me to destruction.

When I totally surrendered my life to God and offered myself as a living sacrifice, I was not depressed anymore. I did not go to a counselor, I was free when I made that conscience decision to follow God with my conduct, life, behavior, and reactions. There is nothing wrong with going to a godly counselor for instructions and help. However, try God first and

He will lead you to someone if you need it. I did not need a counselor, I just needed to choose who I will serve. I needed to choose how I was going to live my life. I had to decide if I was going to do things God's way or my way. Believe me; I talked with Him about my decision. It seems as if others were getting away with things I could not get away with anymore. Things that were not listed in the Bible as sins but I could not do them. God's requirement for each of us might include things He reveal, to you on a personal level. We have to know what He required of each of us as we develop our relationship with Him. I got free that day! Praise God!

God could have let me die in my mess but He kept me. I knew that my mom was praying for me and I am very grateful for her. I hope that others who are going through will come to God earlier than I did. I do not mean just to get save. I mean to walk close with Him. I seem unique and strange to others and still do but I have a sense of who I am and Whom I belong to now. I will not trade my life with anyone now because I am free. I have peace and joy. I have a mind to be about my Father's work. I am pretty sure of what I want to do with my life. I want to serve Him. No matter where and when I need to serve, I am available to Him.

That void I talked about earlier within me was for the Spirit of my Lord, not for anyone else or anything else. He filled it when I made that decision. To be honest, that is all I had to do. I just made a decision and He did the rest. He interfered when I tried to go wrong. He sent a word to me when I needed one for any reason. God filled the "empty" place in my soul. He filled the "empty" place in my life. He connected my spirit with His Spirit.

He is my only God. He is the God of all creations. He has a plan for all of us and the plan will lead us to our rewards from Him. His plan will take us to different locations while we are using different gifts but the same Spirit and the same God is leading us.

**SCRIPTURES:**

Therefore if anyone is in Christ, he is a new creation; old things have passed away; behold all things have become new. II Corinthians 5:17 (NKJV)

Stand fast therefore in the liberty by which Christ has made us free and do not be entangled again with a yoke of bondage. Galatians 5:1 (NKJV)

For unto us a Child is born, unto us a Son is given; and the government will be upon His shoulder. And His Name will be called Wonderful, Counselor, Mighty God, Everlasting Father, Prince of Peace. Isaiah 9:6 (NKJV)

Thank You, Lord, for liberty.
Thank You, Lord, for being my Counselor.

# A Journey Back Home

## January 2013

I remember when I was young. My siblings called me black, smut pot, chocolate, and ugly. I thought I was the ugliest person in the world. I will admit, I was not beautiful or pretty. I felt rejected and worthless because of those statements. I felt no one could love me other than my mom and dad.

Later, I was in a couple of beauty contests and I felt the classmates were just using that opportunity to "pick" at me. I felt like I was in a movie where the students set up an unattractive girl for a big fall. I won my senior beauty contest. I believe my ability to answer the question got me the crown. I knew it was not my beauty.

I met many nice-looking guys who treated me like a queen. I felt I was ugly and not worthy of a relationship with a good-looking guy so I did not take the relationships seriously. I felt they were in the relationships for my body only so my agenda was to use them while they were using me. I have to be honest now; I messed up some relationships because of my "low" opinion of myself.

Sometimes my siblings would call me black and my dad would try to make me feel better by saying "the blacker the berry, the sweeter the juice." He tried to make me feel good but I felt he was validating what they said about me. Thank you, daddy, for trying.

I took that feeling with me a long time. They said my fingers and toes are ugly too. I would not wear sandals with open toes until I was in my late 30's. I was a mess and I put that on everyone I had a relationship with until a change came in my relationship with my heavenly Father.

After I got in the military, I began to change the way I was thinking about myself. I looked in the mirror and saw a beautiful ebony princess starring back at me. I realized I did not look like they told me when I was young. I will admit that I was not a child that if a person saw me they would stop in their steps to comment on my beauty but I was not "dog food" either.

That day I also realized I do not have to settle for less. I was the main focus of jokes when I was younger. If only they knew how much I cried because of the jokes and insults. I felt I was not as important as they were because I was not light skin and pretty.

I was depressed for years. I would sleep all day and get up only when necessary. I put on a good "front" so they would not know the hurt in my heart. I thought about suicide many times but I did not want to feel any pain. And I did not want to hurt my mother. I knew she loved me no matter what happened. She loves me no matter how I look.

The mirror let me see the physical part of me as an ebony princess. My spirit and soul were renewed when I surrendered to God. I did not need a counselor or someone to validate me. I went to God and He helped me through it all. Like it says in Isaiah 9:6, His name is Counselor. I am not depressed anymore. I feel complete and whole. I am wonderfully made and totally sold out to Him. All I can say to everyone is trust God and surrender to Him. Give yourself to Him totally. Do not listen to "man" but to God.

I will say to everyone who is teasing their siblings and others children: DO NOT CALL ANYONE NAMES THAT ARE NOT TO LIFT THEM UP! You can hurt a person in a way that will leave a scar for life. There are shooting in schools because students are getting bully. The students are calling them unpleasant names and teasing each other. You might be teasing the person who will hire you one day. You might be teasing the person God will use to lay hands on you and pray for your healing.

## SCRIPTURES:

Owe no one anything except to love one another, for he who loves another has fulfilled the law. For the commandments; you shall not commit adultery, you shall not murder, you shall not steal, you shall not bear false witness, you shall not covet and if there is any other commandment, are all summed up in this saying, namely, you shall love your neighbor as yourself. Love does no harm to a neighbor; therefore love is the fulfillment of the law. Romans 13:8-10 (NKJV)

Remind them to be subject to ruler and authorities, to obey, to be ready for every good work, to speak evil of no one, to be peaceable, gentle, showing all humility to all men. Titus 3:1 (NKJV)

Thank You, Lord, for my healing. I am not depressed or oppressed. I am full of joy and peace.

# A Brief Journey Back

## February 2, 2013

I remember an incident that happened to me when I was younger. I do not want to hurt anyone with these words but the incident is true. That person I believe has changed. I pray someone can get a blessing from this page. This journey will talk about low self-esteem, pain, fear, revenge, unforgiveness, and forgiveness.

I remember one day one of my exes put his hands around my neck and squeezed. I did not fight back this time like I had often done. I wanted to see how long he was going to do it. Well, he did it until it frightened him. I limped down and my eyes went back into my head, he said. He thought he killed me. He told me it was my fault because I did not fight back. He told me that I was crazy for not fighting back. I thought that would make him stop. This is the revenge. I wanted him to do enough that he would pay for it. I even thought, that if he killed me, his life would be destroyed. It sounds really crazy now. But thank God for renewing the spirit of my mind. I could have died that day.

At that time, I went from fighting to resentment and developed a hard-heart toward him. I wanted him to die. I do not understand how he thought I could love him and make love to him after he fought me. Yes, after the fight, he wanted to make love. I was full of resentment and anger but he wanted what he wanted at the time. I laid there crying and throwing up afterward many times.

I remember him fighting me because I did not want to make him coffee. He fought because I did not want to have sex with him after he fought me. I believe that he did not know that the fighting went beneath the physical but to the emotions and spirit. Some many of us are abused physically, mentally, and verbally daily. I went through it. But he said he loved me. I believe it was possession more than love.

One thing really surprises me is that he claims that he does not remember any of those things. He claims, today, that I hit him first. I know that was not true because I never hit anyone first. I would walk away from him and that would send him into a rage. I would get smart with him and that would send him into a rage.

The main point, ladies and gentlemen, is that no one has the right to hit anyone. If she will not listen, stop talking. Your wife or girlfriend does not have you there for a daddy but for a mate. If you cannot find a way to communicate with her, please go and get some help or just move on. Communication is very important in all relationships and we have to do a better job at it.

I had low esteem because of my childhood and it continued. Now I know that I am wonderfully made and no one has to validate me. I will tell you that I have forgiven him. It was my job to stay happy and to take care of myself. I should not have placed that responsibility into someone else's hand. I was not ready for that relationship, or any other relationship, at the time. I was a mess and took it into the relationship. If you are not secure in your skin and you get with someone who is not secure in their skin, that will lead to destruction.

If a person is mean and hurt you before you get into a relationship with him or her, you should not take that relationship to another level. The signs are there for most relationships. The signs were not there in the first relationship I went through with a mean and abusive person. I revisited the whole relationship often to see what I missed. He was pleasant and encouraging. But after the next level of our relationship, he turned into another person. I did not take it to the next level in just a few months; we were together for over a year. The second relationship did not go as far as the first one because when he slapped me, I ended the relationship. I did not give him another chance. That was the first and last time he hit me. I was not going to go through that again because I love me. I am a valued person who requires love and kindness.

It is odd how I learned so much from that first time. I had one boyfriend who yelled at me in such a way that I felt he would become violent. So, I remained quiet and let him get it out of his system. I decided that night when I left on the plane the next day to go back overseas he would not see me again. He called overseas and wrote, but I did not respond. I was finished with that scene.

Some people might think that I did not give it a chance but I felt that he was speaking in a violent voice and I was very uncomfortable. I will not make my life a dumping place for dysfunctional "boys". They need to get their emotions and hurts in a place of healing and behind them before I would get involve with any of them.

Most of all, I ***must*** seek God for directions and to show me the truths about anyone I meet. Then I have to follow His directions. Low self-esteem was a major part of my abusive relationship. And I will say that unforgiveness was a major part of my bad choices. But forgiveness is a major part of my peace. Forgiveness is a major part of my love for others. I did not get to the "forgiveness" on my own. It was God who helped me do it. I will not say it was easy but I will say if you ask God to help you forgive someone; He will help you.

Now I have to say this for some people: To forgive someone does not mean to stay in an abusive relationship or in any danger. Take care of your temple that God gave you. I remember a lady who was beaten by her husband for many years and she died as a result. Not because of a fatal blow but the damage from years of abuse on her body. The husband did not get arrested. Her children will not have the pleasure of spending holidays and other days with their mother. The choice to stay in that abusive relationship for years cost her a life with her children and future grandchildren. If love hurts, it is not love!

**Okay, Let us talk about forgiveness!**

Unforgiveness will keep you in bondage and make it hard to get closer to God. If we let God move on our behalf, we will have more liberty in our hearts and minds. Forgiving is not a suggestion or a request but a must in the Word of God. It is written in the Bible that we forgive one another as we want God to forgive us. I felt free and as if a heavy substance was lifted off my shoulder when I forgave those who did me wrong.

We are not property, we are humans. We are to be loved, respected, and acknowledged. We have to respect others, love others, and notice others. To notice means to acknowledge that a person's needs and feelings are worth acknowledging and respecting.

Most of all, love yourself and get pass the hurts and pains from your past. The enemy (devil) used someone to take your childhood or your young adulthood but do not let him take your future. Today is a good place to start; today is a present so take advantage of the present God gave you.

**Scripture:**

Bearing with one another, and forgiving one another, if anyone has a complaint against another; even as Christ forgave you, so you also must do. Colossians 3:13 (NKJV)

Thank You, Lord, for Your protection through those years.

Thank You, Lord, for giving me a forgiving heart and forgiving me even when I did not deserve it.

# Journey Seeking Answers

**February 5, 2013**

I do not have much income but I know that it is all good. I feel that I should be doing something. The shift in my life is for a reason but God only knows the reason. I feel as if it is right in my face but I cannot see it at the moment. This might be hard for some to understand but others might understand the state I am in now. I might be in the wilderness or a valley. We cannot lose faith no matter where we are. We have to understand that the enemy will distract us if we get anxiety, so stay focused even in the valley.

I am going to keep moving and keep doing what I do. I will continue to teach, worship, and praise. I still feel as if something is missing. I feel that I am not doing everything I am supposed to do. I am seeking answers from God. I am seeking answers through prayers and the Word but nothing is clear at the moment. When you feel as if you are not sure where you are going or doing, that is the time to ask God to lead you. I asked for truth to be revealed to me. God sent Abram on a journey without Abram knowing where he was going. Abram went without knowing the plan of God. I need to be just as obedient as Abram. I must follow God's directions. In John 1:43, Jesus told Philip to follow Him. We have to follow Him through the Holy Spirit.

So, I just put the whole armor of God on and wait for further directions. I am a living sacrifice for God; this is my reasonable service. This temple belongs to God and He will use it to glorify Himself.

### Scriptures:

The counsel of the Lord stands forever, the plans of His heart to all generations. Psalm 33:11 (NKJV)

But I am like a green olive tree in the house of God; I trust in the mercy of God forever and ever. I will praise You forever, because You have done it;

and in the presence of Your saints I will wait on Your name, for it is good. Psalm 52:8-9 (NKJV)

I beseech you therefore brethren by the mercies of God that you present your bodies a living sacrifice, holy, acceptable to God which is your reasonable service. Romans 12:1 (NKJV)

Thank You, Lord, for using me to fulfill Your plan. I am Your child and I am willing to do Your will.

# A Rainy Morning Journey

February 23, 2013

Feeling a little sick today. I thought I was feeling better but I am not. The rain has been coming down for a couple of days now. I had a desire to go out and do something but the rain stopped that move. The desire is there but I do not want to get in the rain. Can you imagine that in our lives we want to do something but the enemy stops us? We do not want to deal with the struggles so we play it safe and do nothing.

I guess my life is like that sometimes. I have a desire to do something and go places but issues and problems keep me at a standstill. I got to get past the rain (struggles). Drive through it and keep moving no matter what happens.

Rain, rain, the grass will grow. The lakes will fill up again.

Rain, rain, my faith will grow. My passion for Him will manifest again.

Let Your Spirit rain down on me. The rain can keep you humble and let you know that God is God. He does not have to worry about defeat or problems. He is the only One who has all power and knows all things. The thorn in our flesh is to show us that we are human and need Him. The issues in our lives are to help us trust Him and depend on Him only.

Do not hate the rain but embrace it to a point that you can see the Lord's work in it. When we want to do something and the rain comes, we seem to lose our excitement about doing it. Keep the excitement and glorify our Lord in all that we do.

**Scriptures:**

But God, who is rich in mercy, because of His great love with which He loved us, even when we were dead in trespasses, made us alive together with Christ (by grace you have been saved), and raised us up together and made us sit together in heavenly places in Christ Jesus. Ephesians 2:4-6 (NKJV)

My brethren count it all joy when you fall into various trails, knowing that the testing of your faith produces patience. James 1:2-3 (NKJV)

Thank You, Lord, for Your blessings. Rain down on me and let Your will be done.

# A Quiet Journey

**February 28, 2013**

I have been sick now for over a week. It was all quiet time. Things are crazy but mostly in my head. My soul is at peace with God. I have to trust God. I have to believe that He has my best interest in mind. Jeremiah 29:11 says, He knows His plan for me.

I had a "revelation" today. I was leading a congregation. WOW! If I am on the wrong track, I will believe God will show me. I want to be on track and stay on the right track so God can be glorified. I saw the vision or revelation but God will make it come to pass. I am aware of false visions from the enemy, so I do not get caught up in a vision so much that I try to make it happen. I wait until God brings it to pass. I just obey Him and watch Him work. To be honest, it is not my desire to lead a congregation. But my desire is to do His will.

I love the Lord and I thank Him for saving me. I was a mess in the world and I do not want to be a mess in the kingdom. I do not want to be going in circles in this life. I did that in the world before salvation. That is why I am always seeking His directions.

I do not know if it was a false "revelation" from the enemy or a "revelation" from God. But I do know that whatever His plan is for me, the Lord will fulfill it. The Lord will equip and train me to do the task. I do not have to worry. I also know that I am moving forward in the Lord. Praise God!

Please have Your way in my life. Glorify Yourself through me. Teach me so I can teach Your people.

### Scriptures:

But seek first the kingdom of God and His righteousness and all these things shall be added to you. Matthew 6:33 (NKJV)

Blessed are those who hunger and thirst for righteousness for they will be filled. Matthew 5:6 (NKJV)

For I know the thoughts that I think toward you, says the Lord, thoughts of peace and not of evil, to give you a future and a hope. Jeremiah 29:11 (NKJV)

Thank You, Lord, for guiding me.

# Faith Journey

## April 10, 2013

I could not forget to write about the leap I made on December 31, 2012. I made a couple of entries referring to it earlier. I left my job to go and teach God's Word full time. I felt a pull in my spirit to do it and the more I tried to ignore "it", the more it let me know it was there. Then I heard a voice directing me to make the move. Yes, I asked questions about my bills and what would become of me. It might seem crazy to many and believe me, I felt a little discomfort at first. But when I said yes to God, I got peace. When I tried to get nervous or even fearful, I just had peace. It is hard to explain but I had to do it and I believe God is taking me to that 'purpose". This is the third calling. He called me to step out and do this. Now I just have to let Him lead me through it.

Sometimes things get tight but I have to trust Him and know that He is doing this and not me. I teach about faith and now it is time for me to live it. I have to live what I preach. Right? Material things are temporary but our souls will live forever. I have to focus on the eternal things and know that the people need the truth. They need God's truth. I am available and willing to give that truth as God gives it to me. He is the center of my life and I am nothing without Him. I sometimes hope that someone will understand what I am talking about and feeling.

God said that He will take care of my needs and He will provide for me. I have to feed on His faithfulness. I have to commit my way to Him. I have done it and now I have to take the faith journey to glorify Him. Others will see how He alone took care of me and how He is using me to teach the people. All glory goes to the Lord who knows what we need.

I will admit that there are tears and more tears. But I have to say that tears were there when I was working. The bills were behind when I was working. But the peace was not there when I was working. The assignment was over and I tried to stay but I had to leave. He is not a man and He cannot lie.

## Scripture

So Jesus answered and said, "Assuredly, I say to you, there is no one who has left house or brothers or sister or father or mother or wife or children or lands, for My sake and the gospel's, who shall not receive a hundredfold now in this time.... Mark 10:29-30 (NKJV)

Thank You, Lord. You look beyond my faults and use me to serve Your people. Glorify Yourself!

# A Few Dark Nights Journey

## April 29, 2013

Last week my electricity was turned off. I tried to keep it a secret so I would not get pity from others. I do not mind if they pray for me but some might want to give just because of pity and not because it was led by God to bless me. One might say there is no difference but there is. I want God to work through people. That way, He will get the glory and they will receive what it is He is trying to complete in them. Well the lights were off when I got home, I believe this was on Tuesday. At first I panicked and it felt like something had hit me. Then I went to the bank and got my last $100.00. While I was calling to turned back on, I felt in my spirit that I should not do it. So, I did not pay it. I had to use it to go and do something that was part of my ministry. At the time, I did not know that but I just followed the Spirit. Since I do not have much in the refrigerator, it was easy to take care of those items. I asked a friend to store them for a few days. The excuse I used was that the refrigerator was not working. I did not lie. It was not working. I could see that she was thinking about that because I stay in an apartment and they would fix it or give me another one. I asked God to take the thoughts away from her so she would not ask me for more information.

After the second day, a male friend called and asked how I was doing. I replied that I was surviving and that it's all good. He called back saying that I was not telling him everything. He asked if I had food in the house. I told him the situation and I asked that he not pay the bill for me. I told him, "I am doing fine and I am going to see why this happened at this time." One might say because I did not pay the bill, but I say because the Lord allowed it to happen. I have not paid the bill before at the due date and it was not turned off. So, I stayed in the house with no lights or air. That was fine because I do not get hot too often. I have about four battery operated candles in the apartment. I tried to use them but I did not need them. The light from the pole outside shone so bright in my rooms, especially in my bedroom. The first thing I thought about when I got home and the power was off was that I would not be able to look at television while I was in bed. I always kept it on while I slept. I thought that was going to be hard for me. The first night I played a DVD on the laptop and the battery died. Now, no noise at all in the house and it was strange for me. I tossed and turned for a few minutes. Oh, I cried also for a few minutes. At first it was a "feeling sorry for myself" cry then it turn into a "thank you Lord for loving me" cry. My mind was racing with thoughts and I could not stop it. I believe that is why I kept the television on, to focus it to something until I slept. Then I asked God to ease it and let me have a peaceful sleep. He did it! I woke up refreshed and grateful. I felt Him in another way I could not explain. I talked with Him more and not about turning the power on. I talked with Him about who He is in my life and how He works things out for my good. I had peace and was willing to keep the power off for a few more days. But, living in an apartment, I knew that I could not do that because of the policy. However, God worked it out. My friend blessed me with the money when I went home. She would not let me open it until I got home because she knew I would not accept it.

When the lights were off, I saw something in the spiritual life I must share with others. In the Word, you will find in John that the darkness cannot comprehend the light. The darkness cannot overtake the light. I saw that the darkness cannot over take the light because the light that shined in the window was bright, even though it was not in the apartment, like the darkness. I also saw that while I am in a dark place, the Light is within me and He will prevail. I saw that no matter how dark it might be, the Light will be there and give me what I need at the time. I needed peace and to rest. I got it. Some did not understand and to be honest I did not either. But before I went to church that Sunday, I asked God for the significance of the whole matter. When I got to church, He revealed it through the pastor's message.

I was in a dark place in my life. But the Light was there and He would not leave me alone. He gave me rest in that place. I can do without the provision of man but I cannot do without Him. He is there and will always be there with me. I have to just look at Him and know that He is going to be there no matter what comes in my life. That was a "wow" moment for me. Now I have to take the garments off that hold me down and follow Him. I have to cry out to Him like the blind man did when Jesus was passing by. I have to continue to cry until He calls me to come. Look at Luke 18:35-43 and see that Christ asked him what he wanted Him to do for him. Sometimes we just have to tell Him what we want of Him and receive it.

This time in my life is to get me to the next level of my services in God. I will admit, it does not feel good but it feels doable. God will guide me and lead me through this time of my life. I believe that He loves me and He will keep His promise to provide what I need. I also believe what He says in Psalm 37: 3-4. I trust in the Lord and I feed on His faithfulness. I have to because He is all I have to feed on. The psalm continues to say that He will give me the desires of my heart. There are some things I have to do first and I am trying to do them. Commit my way to the Lord.

The light went out at 422 but the Light did not go out. The power went out at 422 but the Power did not go out. I spent more time with my Father and I loved it.

## Scripture

Wait on the Lord and keep His way and He shall exalt you to inherit the land. Psalm 37:34a (NKJV)

Thank you, Lord, for knowing what is best for me.

# Suicide Journey

**May 1, 2013**

I have not thought about suicide since I left Virginia. It was brought to my mind by the enemy today. I used to think about doing it many times when I was on the island. But I always thought about how it would hurt my mother so much. I did not want to hurt her that much. I believe that if she was not living, then I would have done it. When I was young, I thought about killing myself many times. I felt that everyone in the family was normal and worth something. I was just there; I did not know who I was and what I was created to do in this world. As a child, I wondered why I was born and what I was supposed to do here. I mentioned before how alone if felt as a child and empty.

Well, today on the way to Bible study, the idea came in my head to kill myself and I know who put it there. I know it was the enemy and I dismissed the thought. When I got to church, they prayed against the suicide spirit. The person who was praying was talking about the rate of suicide might double this year because at least seventeen people have already committed suicide in town. Some of them were children. I just thank God that I have His power in me. I recognized the enemy for trying to plant it in my spirit. I am a child of the Most High God and I am going to live and live an abundant life.

I rebuke that suicide spirit in every city I enter. My God will fill His people with joy and peace. Lord, fill their hearts with praises and remove that suicide spirit. Whatever distresses the people, please send them help.

**Scriptures:**

Therefore, submit to God. Resist the devil and he will flee from you. James 4:7 (NKJV)

Finally brethren, whatever things are true whatever things are noble, whatever things are just, whatever things pure, whatever things are lovely, whatever things are of good report, if there is any virtue and if there is anything praiseworthy-meditate on these things. The things which you learned and received and heard and saw in me, these do and the God of peace will be with you. Philippians 4:8-9 (NKJV)

Thank You, Lord, for keeping my mind on You. I thank You for protection against the enemy.

# Heads Up Journey

**June 20, 2013**

This entry is a few weeks late. They repossessed my vehicle a couple of weeks ago. It is gone and they want money to get my items out of it. Let me tell you about the days that led up to the incident. God is real and knows everything. A couple of days before they got my vehicle, God showed me that something was about to happen. Someone might say that was not a reason to praise God but I did. You see, praise is the weapon I had to deal with this issue. I praised Him for a couple of days non-stop. I did not understand but I knew something was going to happen. God set me free from the bondage. Yes, I am without a vehicle now but I feel free. I could not get sad or disappointed because I praised already for the peace and joy of being His child. I got joy in the morning. Joy came because God kept me and He did not allow it to trouble my spirit. God could have fixed the situation so that I kept the vehicle but He did not and I cannot say why. All I know is that He is good and full of grace. His grace was sufficient for the time and I praise Him for that moment.

Things will not always work out the way we expect it to be worked out. We have to trust that God knows what He is doing and that He is preparing us for something else. He is going to let it work out for my good. I am called for a purpose and I love Him so I know I am more than a conqueror.

It might look as if I am getting demoted to everyone, but I am being promoted in God's kingdom. Material things are leaving but my relationship and my trust in Him are increasing. God is the center of my being. I am nothing without Him. I cry when I think about Him not being in my everyday life. Not because of things but because of peace, joy, love, spirit, and my sanity.

I made a conscious decision to live the lifestyle He wants. I have the Holy Spirit to guide me and keep me in that area that He delights in my life. It seems foolish to some but others understood what was going on from the start. When you answer the third call, your life will change and you are more obedient to His will. I am His and only His. He is my Provider. To some it looks as if He is not providing much but a transition is taking place and the miracle will happen soon, in His time. That vehicle was a burden to me and He removed the burden. Praise God. I can praise Him in my subtractions as well as the additions.

**Scripture:**

But the Lord is with me as a mighty Awesome One. Jeremiah 20:11a (NKJV)

Thank You, Jehovah, for showing me the hand of the enemy.

# Storms of Life Journeys

July 5, 2013

A few days ago, a friend and I were traveling. We ran into several storms. We drove for over an hour trying to make it to our destination through the storms. It is always amazing how God can use the simple, practical things of our lives to give us spiritual revelations. The prophets in the Old Testament had to do practical things to bring messages to the nations sometimes. If we look, we would see God is showing us things through the foolishness of this world.

We were traveling and drove into a heavy storm. It was raining really hard and we could not see the road very well. She asked if I could see the road because she could not see it. I told her that I could only see the lines reflecting so I followed them so I could stay in the lane. Some times in our lives, we cannot see the direction God is leading us but we have to follow the Light. We have to follow the Holy Spirit and He will show us. We traveled a few miles in that storm. We have to push through our storms even when they are hard and heavy. We have to just follow the Light through our storm and it will be alright. After traveling a few miles, we drove in a little rain. During that time, we just praised God for the safe travel to that area. Even though we were still in the rain, we were grateful it was not as bad as before. Praise and worship can ease the burdens in our lives.

We praised our way out of the heavy storm and in the small one. For about fifteen minutes, we traveled with no rain. Life is like that! We can be in serious problems and get out of it. Then get into a small problem and get out of it. And then have no problems at all. We have to still praise Him and that is what we did each time. After all the different measures of rain, we got back into heavy rain again. This storm was much worse than any of them tonight. It was very dark for seconds. I had to tell her that I could not see for a few seconds. I lost my sight for a few seconds. We can lose sight on this journey but we have to know that He can see and know all things. We can go through so much on our Christian journey that we lose our way. We have to go back and repent. Get back on the right path! I was amazed at how quickly He brought back my sight and the darkness was cleared away by light. Stay abided in Him and His Word and the darkness cannot dwell in you. Darkness cannot comprehend Light.

In between those storms was an encounter with an irrigation system. The water was spraying on the car as we passed it. I knew that it was different but I could not identify what it was at the time. The water was not a storm and I felt it was just there to distract me. I knew the water did not fall on the car right. It reminded me of the devil. He will try to put you in a storm that God did not approve. I am a child of the Most High God and He will have to approve of my storms. I rebuked the enemy quickly and let him know that this storm was not going to take place in my life. We got out of it very quickly. Afterward, we saw it was the irrigation system. We can rebuke the devil of his tricks and plans. We have to rebuke some storms with the authority Christ has given us. Glory to God our Father who is in control of our lives. The enemy's storms cannot destroy you but they can distract you. Be aware of those distractions.

After the distraction, we drove for about ten miles with no rain. It was clear, but when we got very close to home; we traveled through another storm. As we approach the end of an assignment that the Lord gives us, we will notice a storm will come to try to get us distracted or to stop the assignment. Do not stop or lose focus before you complete it. The last storm was longer and more intense. It lasted for more than twenty-two miles. Water was high on the road and we had to drive slow. Some vehicles passed me going very fast. In life, it will seem as if some people will pass you very fast in their ministry and careers. But we have to take the pace God set before us. We are following the same God, the same Spirit but we have different ministries. They went their way and I went my way at a different pace.

God will lead us all in the same place at the end. We will be with Him. We cannot complain about that. In our storms and in our sunshine days, we are guided by Him. We have to praise Him in all the situations in our lives including sunshine and rain.

## Scriptures:

Indeed, before the day was, I am He; and there is no one who can deliver out of My hand; I work and who will reverse it? Isaiah 43:13 (NKJV)

Do not fear, nor be afraid. Have I not told you from that time, and declared it? You are My witnesses. Is there a God besides Me? Indeed, there is no other Rock; I know not one. Isaiah 44:8 (NKJV)

Thank You, Lord, for keeping Your promises to us. I love You and again I trust You.

# A Thankful Journey

**August 26, 2013**

I had an encounter with an old friend which left me examining myself. A lust spirit was very strong on him but I did not realize it until now. I thought it was old feelings that we had from years ago but now I know it was a lust spirit. He suggested that we get together but I did not meet with him. (Thank You, Holy Spirit) I will admit, ladies, it was a little struggle not to meet him. Glory to God, He kept me from going. I have to say He will intervene and keep you if you want to be kept. Yes, I am an ordained minister and I struggled at that moment. I love the Lord and I put the relationship I have with God before all my relationships. That is what helps me to make the right choices. Now that person is in trouble from yielding to that lust spirit. I pray that he will learn from his mistakes and seek God for strength. I have to thank God for helping me make godly choices. I could have been in a situation with a married man and fornicating. Sin is sin.

No one said it would be easy but God did promise to be there and never leave us. He proves it to me over and over again. He protects me and keeps me. Like the scripture said His grace is sufficient for us. I have had a relationship with a married man, a man on the down low, and guys who were cheating with other women. I could have diseases that could have destroyed me. I could have been a big mess from those relationships. I did not want to admit this to anyone but I am writing what is deposited in my spirit to write. So now you know more about my soiled past. Thank God for grace. I once was lost but now I am found. God's grace protected me. I made many wrong choices trying to find myself and believe me when I say I am not perfect. I make better choices with the help of the Holy Spirit, most of all I make godly choices. God will help us but remember that He wants us to make a conscious decision to follow Him. Do not practice sinning.

I am just like all humans; I come short. I try to make less mistakes and decisions that will cost me more than I can pay. Weigh out the results of our actions and then make a choice. Believe me; the piper will come for his pay. Seek God and He will help you make decisions but the final choice is yours (Adam).

**SCRIPTURES:**

And the Word became flesh and lived among us and we beheld His glory. The glory as of the only begotten of the Father, full of grace and truth. John 1:14 (NKJV)

And He said to me, My grace is sufficient for you, for My strength is made perfect in weakness. II Corinthians 12:9 (NKJV)

Thank You, Lord, for Your grace and mercy.

# A Past Journey

**October 24, 2013**

I thought about something that I believe happened when I was very young. I believe it happened when I was very, very young. I have a small memory about it. I could be wrong but this flashes in my mind often. I never asked anyone about this. I am not sure if anyone knows if it happened or not. I used to see things happen to other people so this could be someone else's problem I saw. Stay with me on this page; it sounds crazy.

This is the scene I saw often: I was young and my dad was working at a factory. My mom was not home at the time. A friend of the family touched me inappropriately. I am not sure who it was but I know it was a male figure that I saw in my vision. I really believe it was a friend of the family but I am not sure. The male was supposed to be going to the restroom but he stopped in our room. It happened once I believe. During my marriage, I experienced flashbacks often. I tried to repress the vision but I could not. I tried to forget it but it comes to me often.

For some reason, I had to put this in the book is to minister to someone. If you were touched inappropriately, please get healing from it because it could cost you problems later. If you are dealing with past events that are not settled yet, please face them and get your healing. You need to live and live the abundant life.

Many of our issues and decisions we deal with today come from our past. So, let us move on to a bigger and better future. Forgive that person who hurt you and heal. If this thing happened to me, I am thankful that God stopped it and that it did not continue. Do not let the enemy destroy your future. If you are hurting someone, please stop and get help. I ask God to reveal the truth now. It is more than just touching a person physically, this thing goes much deeper. Seeds are planted that grow into anger, low self-worth, and many other issues. You can destroy someone's life if you hurt them. If we think about how we will feel if we were treated badly, maybe we will stop hurting others.

**SCRIPTURES:**

Therefore having these promises, beloved, let us cleanse ourselves from all filthiness of the flesh and spirit, perfecting holiness in the fear of God. II Corinthians 7:1 (NKJV)

Confess your trespasses to one another and pray for one another that you may be healed. James 5:16 (NKJV)

Thank You, Lord, if You protect me from a continuous abuse.

# A Journey to the Big Apple

**November 2, 2013**

I remember one of my trips to New York and it was an event to remember. The twin towers were already destroyed the first time I went there. I saw many of the results from that terrible day. The buildings nearby were damaged but still standing. The mood of the people who experienced the tragedy were damaged. At ground zero; many people were still talking about that day when the United States was attacked on their soil. I never had a problem getting to New York but I had a hard time leaving both times. It was a challenge leaving and not because I did not want to leave. Both times, I was delayed by the weather and/or the plane.

We stayed at the airport for an hour waiting to board the plane. The weather was bad on the east coast so we had to stay in the airport until the weather cleared. After we boarded the plane, we sat on the plane for at least another hour because the weather was still bad. When the weather finally cleared, we had to remain on the runway because the navigation system went out on the plane.

"Now this is getting critical," I began to think. The navigation system is very important to fly a plane and I was a long way from home. I was glad they found the problem before we got into the air. Thank You, Lord. We sat on the plane for an hour and a half waiting for the navigation system to be fixed. Now I am a little worried about them fixing it correctly before we leave. I did not want that thing to go out while we were in the air. We know people do not always do it right the first time. I felt like we were sitting ducks on the runway while planes were coming and going. I will admit, I began to worry. Yes, a child of the Most High God, was worrying.

Now, I have another problem sitting on the plane. I did not like to be in small places. One might say I have a phobia of small spaces. I turned the air on over my head and pretended I was in a larger place. I fooled my mind for a little. But soon my heart began to beat fast.

The enemy began to speak to me because he knew I was fearful. I remember leaning forward in my seat looking out of the window. I pretended I was outside of the plane and ignored the voice of fear in my head. He was saying that I would die today. Wow!

After a few seconds, I came to myself. Just like the prodigal son in the bible came to himself. I told the enemy that I am in a win-win situation. If I die, I will be with God. I will not have to worry about being sick or bills anymore. I will not have to worry about dying or crying anymore. My strength became to come back. I continued to tell him that if I die, the women at the church will have a praise party and someone will come to know God. I began to praise God for who He is and how He loves me. I did not ask God for life or anything else. I just praised Him. I was thanking God and the fear left. The enemy left. Submit to God and resist the devil and he will flee. ***That is scripture.***

Then the Holy Spirit said that I would not die yet because the promises God made to me have not come to pass. I began to laugh. The Spirit of God did not speak until I began to praise God. God did not give us the spirit of fear but a Spirit of power, love, and sound mind. I had three concerns and one enemy that fed me fear. I was concerned about the weather, the navigator system, and the small space. I have one God who came and conquer all three when I praise Him.

I do not have to tell you that God got me home safely. He protected me through many dangerous situations. He is our Protector. Some of my classmates were on the plane and they were fearful also. I remember after everything cleared, the sun began to shine. It was so beautiful and it was shining directly on me. One of my classmates was talking to me about the trip. I told him to leave me alone because I am talking directly to the Father. The other classmate agreed. They noticed the light on me and got excited also. God reminded me that He is the Light.

This practical experience showed me that God is still in control. It also let me know that He hears our prayers and praises. We are in a battle often with the enemy in our minds. He will attack us through our minds. We have to know what God says about us. The joy of the Lord is our strength.

We need to know that God has a place for us when we leave this place. Do not give the enemy your peace. Just praise God for the home He has prepare for us to go to one day. Praise Him for watching over you.

**SCRIPTURES:**

O death where is your sting? O Hades, where is your victory? The sting of death is sin and the strength of sin is the law. But thanks be to God who gives us the victory through our Lord Jesus Christ. I Corinthians 15:55-57 (NKJV)

You will keep him in perfect peace, whose mind is stayed on You, because he trusts in You. Isaiah 26:3 (NKJV)

Thank You, Lord, for grace. Thank You for being our Protector, Light, and Salvation

# Journey of Death

**December 13, 2013**

What a feeling! These last few days have been a ride. I did not know if I was going or coming. I feel at peace but I feel as if something is missing. I began a self-examination. Sometimes we have to examine ourselves. Look at Galatians 6:4 and meditate on it.

I have to check and see if I am holding on to unforgiveness or uneasy feelings toward anyone. I noticed I could not hug someone in the church. I asked God to forgive me for holding to something that is not of Him. But I still do not know what the feeling is about toward that person. I do not know of anything she has done to me. So I have to ask God to reveal it or just move it. I know I love her and all the others in the church. I do not worry about how people feel about me. I love them and that is what's important. I do not like feeling this way toward anyone so I have to give it to God and make an effort to show her love. If there is something that my spirit feels and I am reacting because of it, then I want to know what it is. So I ask God to reveal all truth.

It is easy to let a thing go if you know what is happening. But I do not know of anything she has done and I do not understand why I am feeling this way. It bothers me and I want it to cease. God is love and He lives in me. I love God and His people.

I have examined myself for other spirits not of God. I want to live holy and righteous. I want the flesh to die daily and all those desires and selfishness that comes along with the flesh to die also. I bind pride, haughtiness, and any other things not of God. I loose, in the Name of Jesus the Christ, the Spirit of God. I release a humble and godly spirit in this temple.

God is cleaning His temple daily. Daily, the flesh dies. Die to the world, die to sin, and die to selfishness. I have to continue to examine myself. The more I read and hear the Word of God, the more I notice I have not arrived. We are a work in progress. We have to know that we are the clay and we have to be shaped. We have to be shaped in the Potter's Hand so He can use us to be a blessing to someone else. God knows our cracks and our imperfections. He is not surprised about our faults.

**SCRIPTURE:**

My brethren, do not hold the faith of our Lord Jesus Christ, the Lord of glory with partiality. James 2:1 (NKJV)

Thank You, Lord, for showing me what is inside of us.

# A Call Journey

**December 16, 2013**

When God called me into a ministry to teach and pray for His people, I will admit that I was fearful. I was already teaching and was satisfied with that status. But God let me know He was taking me to another level. I suggested that God use my cousin. I know she remembers scriptures and she would be better to speak to the people. I also was having problems pronouncing words. I admit to God that people got on my nerves, especially when they are complaining and doing crazy things. The only thing I heard was, "I called you". Well, I can say God knows what He is doing and we have to trust Him.

Now look at me. I still have problems pronouncing certain words but God's Word goes forward. Now I love people and do not judge their decisions. They have to figure out what works for them. I have compassion for people. I want them to stop hurting.

I did not feel I was worthy to be a minister. I am not worthy of any of God's blessings. But God! God uses ordinary people to do His will. He is using a country girl to go places teaching His Word. A girl with low self-esteem and not sure of who she is. A girl who felt her biological father did not care enough to sacrifice his time to continue to visit her and her siblings. A divorced single mom! God uses a woman to carry His Word and work miracles through her. Some do not believe God will use such a person but He is and He knows what He is doing. God knows we are not perfect. I am not perfect but I am obedient to the best of my ability. I do not practice sin but come short sometimes. I confess those shortcomings and repent.

When I am weary and tired, I praise God. I sing and sing until I feel my strength come back. I want them to see God, not me, when I am teaching. I allow my flesh to die daily so God will be seen in me. My mind, attitude, conduct, and behavior changed since I have been walking on this journey.

I am a new creature in God. The Potter is still molding me so He can use me for His plan.

While I am in the valleys, I will leave those things that are not of God and weighing me down. Now I can climb the mountains without all the hurts, pains, unforgiveness, envy, jealousy, and other evidence of the flesh that could be holding me down. I want to be all God created me to be. He is calling us to love and praise Him. The call to be a minister is a serious calling.

We have to be obedient to Him. He is calling many of us to greater things on this earth. Selfishness and fear can keep us at a level that is not part of our purpose. You are unique and different from others because God has called you for a ministry (service). You think differently from your siblings because God chose you to be the one to carry His Word.

Trust God and do not walk in fear. If He called you, believe me, He will keep you. God made some promises in the Bible. Believe me; He will complete those promises. Seek Him through the Word and prayer. If you notice anything in you that is not right, pray about those things so you can be cleaned.

The whole "circle" of living for God is to obey. Obey Him and you will find joy, peace, love, self-control, gentleness, and all the fruit of the Spirit. Be content where you are in life while you are serving God. You can be satisfied where you are and still move to your promise. If you obey, then He will lead you to the next assignment.

You have to learn to live a humble life. That means to be teachable. Even though you are special and wonderfully made, you do not think of yourself above anyone. We are in the race together and we have to edify each other. We are called to have salvation through Christ. Then we are called for our personal spiritual ministry (service). Next, we are called to go live with our Father.

**Scriptures:**

Listen, my beloved brethren: Has God not chosen the poor of this world to be rich in faith and heirs of the kingdom which He promised to those who love Him? James 2:5 (NKJV)

Though He was a Son, yet He learned obedience by the things which He suffered. Hebrews 5:8 (NKJV)

While through the proof of this ministry they glorify God for the obedience of your confession to the gospel of Christ, and for your liberal sharing with them and all men, and by their prayer for you, who long for you because of the exceeding grace of God in you. Thanks be to God for His indescribable gift! II Corinthians 9:13-15 (NKJV)

Thank You, Lord, for saving me first and then for using me to glorify Your Name.

# A Healing Journey

**December 21, 2013**

I remember when I had hatred in my heart. I will let you know that to hate someone is a sick thing. We think that we hate someone when in fact we only dislike them. Hatred will consume you. I hated that person for doing a bad thing to me. When I first got into the military, I was driving to work daily without remembering anything that happened that day including, the ride to work and back home. All day I would go in the bathroom and cry. Then I would dry my eyes and go back to work. No one knew what I was going through. I received awards for "most production" and did not remember doing the work.

I was walking on base that day, praying that God would take care of that situation. I heard a voice say, "You need to get rid of that hatred in your heart first." That day, God spoke to me. I could not go to a chaplain, He sent me to the church in Chesapeake. That church was used to begin my healing. I attended Bible study and the other services. The members and pastor there showed me love. The mothers acted as a mother to me. The young ladies and men treated me like a sister. The older men treated me like a daughter. I cannot tell you when the hatred left but I know I started working in the church and getting the Word and love I needed at the time.

I began to laugh again. After a few months, I was stationed overseas. The healing continued. The Lord moved in the heart of a friend to give me a Bible. I read it every night, the same scripture, Psalms 51. God was cleaning me from the inside, I did not know that was taking place. I realized I was a sinner and my heart needed cleaning. David said, "Blot out my transgression." I really needed that. I did not want to go out to clubs and be in those "unhealthy" relationships where I was giving my body too freely. I just wanted to read the Bible and think. Yes, think. I cannot remember everything I thought about but I spent lots of times alone and "thinking". No matter what time of night it was, I had to read the scripture. It was as if the Bible was calling my name as it was lying on my desk. I could not go to bed without reading that scripture. Each night the scripture would show me something different. I would feel as if I ate something when I finished reading it. I felt as if I was changing inside. I did not crave the same life style. I began to think differently about people, including the person I hated. I did not react the way I used to in the past. It started with a Word from God. I heard a Word, I ate the Word and I embraced the Word.

**SCRIPTURE:**

But the manifestation….to another faith by the same Spirit, to another gifts of healings by the same Spirit… I Corinthians 12:7-11 (NKJV) Thank You, Lord, for the Word.

# Early Morning Journey

**December 22, 2013**

I remember when I first began this journey; God would wake me up early in the morning. At first, I would stay in bed and try to go back to sleep. Then I realized I was not sleepy and just laid there thinking. I did not understand that God was trying to communicate with me. I know I did not like getting up early at all. But every time I got up and prayed, I felt better all day. I read the Bible and prayed until I felt we finished our time together. I talked with Him and it was our time alone.

Like the dew in the morning, His Spirit was all over me as I talked with Him. The house and community are still early in the morning between 3:30 am – 5:00 am.

How do you know it was God who woke you? Glad you asked. I did not have to use the bathroom. I was not tired. I was not upset about anything. It was as if someone touched me to wake up. It took me several times to get this. As I said before I just did not want to get up. Not because I was tired but because it was 3:30-5:00 in the morning. He showed me things. I saw things about me, my son, my family, co-workers, church members, events about to happened and even people overseas.

After we had our time together as Father and child, I began to do intercessors prayer in the morning too. It's been a while since He woke me up early. Thank you for waking me up this morning. I miss those times together, Father.

God wants your first fruit, which includes your first and your best. Give Him your best offering, such as your time, service, and substance, including money. You will not regret it. It will help you with your growth and relationship with Him.

**Scripture:**

For if the first fruit is holy, the lump is also holy; and if the root is holy, so are the branches. Romans 11:16 (NKJV)

Thank You, Lord, for spending time with me.

# A Nehemiah's Journey

**December 24, 2013**

In the book of Nehemiah, you will see that God has put a burden in his heart for His people. He had a charge to build the walls of Jerusalem and the temple. Nehemiah prayed to God first in chapter 1 before he did anything. He also asked God for favor from a man, the king, to help him with the task.

Nehemiah stayed focused even though people and time was not on his side. He had to get up and build. He did what God told him to do and did it with courage.

We need to understand that we have to stay focused on the purpose that God has for our lives. We have to get up and go to work. Work while it is day because when it gets dark, no man can work. When you die, you cannot work anymore. You are finished, just waiting on God to do the rest of the Book of Revelation. Rise up and work. Faith combined with work is successful. When you work your faith, the reality of your faith will become visible to others.

If you have a ministry to do and times are getting hard, push forward and stay focused on God. He will give you the strength to do it. If He said it would happen; then it will. If He said you are healed, guess what? You are healed. If you want to be sustained, believe me, God will sustain you.

You should do the work and have the faith. God handles the results. Like the psalmist wrote: "A charge to keep I have and a God to glorify." The second stanza has another powerful message, "O may in all my power engaged to do my Master's will." All my power to connect (engage) to do His will. We have a charge, a task, a purpose to keep so we can glorify God. Our calling on our lives should be fulfilled. The psalmist wrote, "My calling to fulfill". So, Rise up and build!

Read Nehemiah and get the revelation you need.

**Scripture:**

Comfort your hearts and establish you in every good word and work. II Thessalonians 2:17 (NKJV)

Thank You, Lord, for blessing the works of my hands.

Thank You, Lord, for guiding me through the valleys.

# A Relationship Journey

December 31, 2013

I remember asking the members of a church how I know that God is talking to me. They gave me several answers. One person said that the enemy will not tell you to do anything good. After I heard many different answers, I was not satisfied with the answers.

I then asked God the question. He will answer your questions. God gave me a practical answer. I was in the church at the moment. God talked to me so clear. This is the illustration He gave me:

My sister and I have always had an intimate relationship. He said that if Weesie was in the other room and I did not know she was there and I heard someone talking that sounds like her, I would say that the voice sounds like my sister's. As the person talks, I would be confident that she is in the other room. Then, the person will begin to laugh and I am even more sure that the person in the room is my sister. Next, the person will use a phrase which I hear her say a lot so I will be most certain that it is my sister. He said I would know it was her because I had spent some intimate time with her, so I know her voice.

If I want to know Him, I need to spend some intimate time with Him. I have to pray to Him and read His Word. I have to spend some time getting to know who He is and His characteristics.

That was a great moment in my life. God uses practical things to show us spiritual things. You should see that in this book. The natural things show us God and His works.

For example:

Ezekiel's wife died. God allowed this to happen to send a message to Israel. (Ezekiel 24:15-27) God told Ezekiel not to mourn nor weep for her death. He could not shed any tears. He had to lament in silence. God wanted Ezekiel to show Israel what He was doing or going to do to them.

The Lord said, "I profane My sanctuary, your arrogant boast, the desire of your eyes, the delight of your soul and your sons and daughters whom you left behind shall fall by the sword." And there will be no mourning or weeping like Ezekiel. But they shall pine away in their iniquities. They should do like Ezekiel and when this comes they will know He is the Lord God.

One day, He used the shower to show me a message. He has been sending a message to me through others saints. You might hear people say that the anointing of God is all on you. Well, what does that mean? I was in the shower and I decided to let the water run down from the top of my head and freely run down my body. I saw a picture of the anointed Spirit of God flowing from the top of my head and down to my feet. God can touch every part of your body. Trust Him; seek Him, and most of all, have a relationship with Him. He will let His Spirit engulf you and flow in and on you.

God is trying to communicate with us daily. We have to listen and be in a place to receive His voice. It is not a loud voice but a small voice in your being. God loves us and He is guiding us through His Spirit. Accept the Holy Spirit and let Him lead you.

God is all over this land. He talks to people in China, Africa, Mexico, Japan, and the United States of America. God speaks through His Word, His Spirit and through other people. Are you listening and available to Him? Moses heard Him speak and so did his brother, Aaron, and his sister, Miriam. Saul heard Jesus speak to Him before his conversion.

**Scriptures:**

My help comes from the Lord, who made heaven and earth. Psalm 121:2 (NKJV)

Then the Lord said to him, Arise and go into the city and you will be told what you must do. Acts 9:6 (NKJV)

Thank You, Lord, for taking the time out to talk with me.

Speak Lord and guide us through this journey.

# A Love Journey

## January 2, 2014

Did you know that God created our personality, not our attitude? Our attitude comes from the past and present events of our lives. For example, the hurt in your past can leave you with an attitude of being bitter and isolated. When people say, a person has a bad attitude, I can guarantee you that the person has been through something that made her attitude like that.

There is a difference between being an introvert and being withdrawn. A person can be born an introvert. When a person is abused, especially as a child, that child will become withdrawn. An introvert does not necessarily clam up or refuse to communicate with certain people. A hurt person will not talk with certain people. For example, if a female has been molested by two males on different occasions, usually she will not socialize and it will be hard for her to socialize with men. We know that this is not absolute but I have seen this pattern with the young ladies, I mentor. Have a relationship with your child and you will know that her attitude has changed. Believe me, it was for a reason.

Sometimes, when you see someone who is angry, please be patient with her. She might have a past that is hard to conquer or a present that is hard to endure. If you are mentor be there to listen to the verbal and nonverbal words of your mentees.

I have seen many "mommy boyfriends" cause anger in children. Mommy, take care of your precious treasures God trusted you to rear. God is looking at you. A child should feel safe in their home more than any place. Where is the love? Compromise your selfishness to give them a safe loving home. Do not leave your boyfriend to do your job.

All this is called love. Love them in your homes. Love them in your schools. Love them when they are hurting and angry. Love is an action word. Take action and love our children, youth, and young adults.

**SCRIPTURE:**

Love suffers long and is kind; love does not envy; love does not parade itself, is not puffed up, does not behave rudely, does not seek its own, is not provoked and thinks no evil. I Corinthians 13:4-5 (NKJV)

Thank You, Lord, for my son and grandsons.

# Lost Direction on the Journey

**January 2, 2014**

I remember in Iceland how the weather could get really bad so quickly. I used to walk to the gym at least six days a week. It was a five to seven-minute walk. I made that walk often with no problems. One day I was in the gym and the weather got so bad before I left. I left in the blowing snow. I had to bend over to keep the snow from getting into my eyes. I knew the direction I was walking because I had done many times. But I was lost. When I realized it had taken so long to get to the barracks, I decided to look at the buildings and see if I recognized any of them. I was on the other side of the base. The walk that usually takes five to seven minutes had become a twenty-minute journey. I did not know which way to go. I had to stand there for a minute and pray. That was a scary feeling. They warned us when we got there that we could get lost in the snow and to travel in pairs in bad weather. I was cold and fearful.

*Revelation:*

We sometimes get off the right path. We once were lost and were going in the wrong direction. God came and put us on the right path. As Christians, sometimes, we still go the wrong way. We lose our directions when times are hard. But we need to come to our right mind. We need the mind of Christ and to get on the right path which God has prepared for us. The prodigal son in the Bible went and spent his money. The Bible says that when he came to himself, he went home. Before he went, he confessed that he was living wrong and in a bad state. He remembered that it was better at his father's house. It is better in our Father's house. It is better in His love, plan, and protection.

Get on the right path. Confess your mistakes and go for the goal.

**Scriptures:**

And of His fullness we have all received and grace for grace. John 1:16 (NKJV)

But grow in grace and the knowledge of our Lord and Savior Jesus Christ. To Him be the glory both now and forever. Amen. II Peter 3:18 (NKJV)

But He gives more grace. Therefore He says: God resists the proud, but gives grace to the humble. James 4:6 (NKJV)

Thank You, Lord, for direction on earth.

# A Place in God

January 3, 2014

Paul said to be content in the state you are in (Philippians 4:11). He did not say to stop trying to be all that God called you to be. He means that whenever you are in your life, praise God for His grace and provisions. I saw what that looks like today.

A dear person to me showed it to me today. He does not have a house or all the material things we think that makes us successful. He has a job with above average pay. He is renting a room. He is separated from his wife and immediate family. He still drinks but not as much as he used to drink. But he has peace. He is in a good place. He said sometimes a little depression comes but he just sits still and gets his mind right. He gives God all the praise for where he is now in his life. Why? Because he has a roof over his head and he has food to eat. He also remembers how hungry and down in the bottom (literally) he was before. "But God," he said, "God took care of me and put me in this stage of my life." He shows love to everyone who wants it. He does not seek who he can bless but he blesses those who are in his presence. He always has a kind word to say if one is there for a person. He does not lie about how he feels. He tells the truth or says nothing if it is not necessary.

He takes one day at a time because he realizes that God will take care of his tomorrow. Because he is not going to church every Sunday or because is known as an alcoholic, some might think he is not saved. But guess what? He is saved. He has salvation! He confesses to everyone that Jesus is Lord of his life. He believes God raised Jesus from the dead. He knows that God has a place for him when he takes his last breath. He loves the Lord and now he knows that God loves him even when he was down and out. A church is across the street from his house and he goes sometimes to worship there.

We can learn from him, "church people". He has love, compassion, and offerings for others. He tries very hard not to cause problems to others. He would rather stay away from you than to cause you harm. Where he stays is just geography. What he drinks is just liquid to digest and dispose. How he lives is eternal. The material state he is in is temporary. Peace is the key for his sleeping and his smiling. Grateful to God is the key to his word of encouragement to others. He is more at peace than many of us (Christians).

**Scripture:**

And the King will answer and say to them, Assuredly, I say to you, inasmuch as you did it to one of the least of these My brethren you did it to Me. Matthew 25:40 (NKJV)

Thank You, Lord, for giving him peace.

Thank You, Lord for having him in my life.

# Making the Journey Even When it is Raining

**January 11, 2014**

As I was traveling to school this weekend, it was raining hard. My journey began with rain and it rained throughout the journey. It was early in the morning and I had to pick up a classmate. I was not sure what exit she was on to meet me and neither was she. I put the street name in the GPS to guide me to the street. The weather was very bad and I had to drive slowly. I got off a couple of exits because they had the city name on them but they were the wrong areas. I continued to drive until I decided to follow the GPS. It led me to the road. It was not talking so I had a hard time following the directions. I had to keep moving so I could get to school.

I finally found my classmate. The weather had cleared up so the journey was a little better. The weather got bad again as we got close to the school. We could not see the road and the GPS was not talking to me. I went to school many months but not in the direction I was coming from today. We drove around in circles until we finally found the school. We were late but the instructor was more concerned about our safety than us being late.

One the way back, we could not find her house. She was confused about the turns and I did not have a clue. The GPS was dead at this time. We drove around almost two hours trying to find her home but it was good. On the way home I decided to go the back way through the small cities. The ride was great and peaceful. I got a chance to reflect on the day. The weather was very clear.

**Revelation:**

We will have to go in the rain, through the storm of our lives to get where God is leading us. The pain and hurts of our lives should not stop us from doing His will and praising Him. We have to stay patient and love others while we are in our storms. The GPS was not talking to me, nor was it working at the end, but God will always talk to us and He will always be available to us through His Spirit. Keep moving forward; the journey is worth the ride. The storms are temporary and the grace of God is more powerful.

God will lead us home and He will direct us to His place. He will not send us in circles, we send ourselves in circles being disobedient. The GPS had no power but God has all power, and will not lose it. Praise God! Go through the rain and make it to your destination.

Each assignment needs to be complete. We cannot stop because something is hard to do. We have to believe and get our strength from the Lord. If He told you to do it then just do it. The journey might be hard but it is doable. God will not ask us to do anything that He has not prepared a way for it to be accomplished. Praise your way through it. Seek His face through it.

Remember God is on this journey with you. You are not alone. He will never leave you or forsake you when times get hard. He will be there to comfort you and guide you. Stay in the Word and be of good courage.

**Scripture:**

For this is God, our God forever and ever; He will be our guide even to death. Psalm 48:14 (NKJV)

Thank You, Lord, for the strength through the rain.

Printed in the United States
By Bookmasters